Runner's World

TRIATHLON TRAINING BOOK

Runner's World

TRIATHLON TRAINING BOOK

by Mark Sisson
with Ray Hosler

Runner's World Books

Library of Congress Cataloging in Publication Data

Sisson, Mark, 1953-
  Triathlon training book.

  Bibliography: p. 138
  1. Triathlon – Training. I. Hosler, Ray, 1952-
II. Title.
GV1060.7.S54   1983   796.4'07   83-4523
ISBN 0-89037-262-4

© 1983 by
Mark Sisson

Anderson World Books, Inc.
1400 Stierlin Road
Mountain View, CA 94043

ON THE COVER: Triathlete Scott Tinley contemplates the
                       upcoming Ironman triathlon from Kailua Pier.
                       (Ray Hosler photo)

Contents

Dedication. vi

Acknowledgments. vii

Introduction ix

Chapter 1: Triathlon: Out of the Twilight Zone

and Into the Limelight 11

Chapter 2: Metamorphosis. 24

Chapter 3: Float, Coast and Shuffle. 30

Chapter 4: Health vs. Fitness 62

Chapter 5: Training Strategy .77

Chapter 6: Workouts and a Plan for

Peak Performance. 81

Chapter 7: In Sickness and in Health 92

Chapter 8: Mind Games. 110

Chapter 9: On Race Strategy, Tactics and

Transition. 116

Bibliography 139

About the Authors 141

Recommended Reading. 142

Dedication

To the athletes and race sponsors, whose foresight, courage and dedication have created for the modernday renaissance athlete a new form of self-expression.

Acknowledgments

If not for Ian Jackson, I would never have become a triathlete. His coaxing and inspirational words convinced me to redirect my interests in competitive sports.

Many of the ideas in this book, and the desire to write it, have come from other athletes, including: John Howard, who taught me to push big gears; Kevin Frampton, whose overall attitude toward training and life finally made me see the light; Paul Clark, whose patience as a coach helped me in swimming; Read Boles, who coined the phrase Float, Coast and Shuffle, among others; Ray Hosler, who suggested that I write a book, and who helped put my training methods into print.

Special thanks to Dave Madison for his bike (instructional) photos, and to Trevor Coppock for the photo of Allison Roe.

Finally, I wish to thank Kim, whose support and encouragement has made all the ups and downs in training and racing a lot more bearable.

Introduction

It seems that the one subject everyone was a qualified expert on at the 1981 Ironman was overtraining. Each of us had stories to tell of nightmarish weeks doing hundreds of training miles while down with a cold or unable to sleep or depressed to near-suicidal levels. Each of us recognized the signs of overtraining, were aware of its effects and yet continued to overtrain right up to the day of the Ironman. Few of us were brave enough at that time to back off and analyze our training schedules. We were afraid that training any less than we were would give someone else the edge and nullify the months of time we had devoted to training for the event.

I was amazed to discover that most of us were in the same position one year later. Many who had turned in substandard performances in 1981, fully aware of having overtrained, returned home to train even harder in an attempt to redeem themselves. I and a few others had decided, or were forced by injury, to apply an objective knowledge of training to that subjective quest for glory. We returned to Hawaii almost ashamed of the low training mileage, but certainly ready for the test. The results of that 1982 race proved to me and a few others that there was more to training for triathlons than just putting in long miles.

When Ray Hosler approached me with the prospect of co-authoring a book on the triathlon, I saw it as my opportunity to share painlessly some of the painful lessons I learned as an athlete. I had at the time decided to take two years off to take care of some of the running injuries that had accumulated during a decade of competition, and felt the book would be a great way to keep me involved in this sport that had come to dominate my life. More important, though, I've felt throughout

9

my competitive career that it's the athlete's obligation to con-
tribute, to put back some of what he has taken out. The athlete
trains hard, and if he's successful, all the glory goes to him. He
frequently forgets that race sponsors, volunteers, supporting
family and friends are the real reasons he is able to compete in
the first place. In this respect, triathletes are probably the most
willing of all athletes to share ideas because the triathlon is such
a new sport. Three cheers to its future.

Mark Sisson
Menlo Park, California
January 1983

1

Triathlon: Out of the Twilight Zone and Into the Limelight

The late Rod Serling, television's mastermind of tales of the bizarre and unusual in *"The Twilight Zone,"* might have been interested in the triathlon. There's nothing unusual about swimming, cycling and running, but who would ever think to combine all three sports into a single event?

The idea of a triathlon was conceived in February 1977 following the awards ceremony of a relay running event in Honolulu. It was intended as a joke. Navy Captain John Collins and some of his military associates are responsible for creating the triathlon, which has, for some, become a private hell of pain. For others it represents another bold step in man's search for the limits of physical endurance — a personal struggle of mind over matter.

The triathlon evolved during an argument, one that is often heard in Hawaii. Captain Collins and friends debated back and forth about which of the state's endurance events was most difficult — the Waikiki 2.4-mile rough-water swim, the Around-Oahu 112-mile bike race or the Honolulu Marathon. Someone in the group suggested combining all three events into a single race. At first everyone laughed, but the idea took on a life of its own. Captain Collins seized the opportunity. He decided to take over the helm of an untested sport in uncharted waters, and immediately impressed a crew to put on the triathlon.

The inaugural race went off on a wet, blustery day in January 1978 on the island of Oahu, where romance, tourists, bikinis

11

and sports share equal billing. Fifteen men — no women — competed. The winner, Southern Californian Gordon Haller, was aptly named an "Iron Man," and so was the race.

Fame was not far behind the Ironman. In 1979, *Sports Illustrated* published a memorable story about the race. In 1980, ABC-TV sent Diana Nyad and Jim Lampley to cover the Ironman for *"Wide World of Sports."* Within three years of its birth, the triathlon had grown to larger-than-life proportions. By 1982, the race had officially become known as the Budweiser Light Hawaii Ironman Triathlon World Championship.

At the February 1982 race, ABC's cameras taped an unforgettable finish of the top two women. The setting was like something out of a dream: A gentle ocean breeze stirred the island's tropical air. In the darkness, cheering crowds lined the streets of Kailua near the finish line. The light from lamps set up to film the race added to the eeriness. Enter Julie Moss to the well-lighted stage. The 23-year-old from Southern California did not think she had a chance to win going into the race, and it was not until well past the halfway point that visions of victory filled her with anticipation — and doubt. Her doubts multiplied as, with each step in the marathon, she lost strength. Finally, in the last quarter-mile, exhaustion set in, and so did rigor mortis. Under the lights of TV cameras and to the exhortations of the crowd, Moss fell, got up, and fell again. Her wobbly legs were like those of a newborn colt. As she started to crawl the last 100 yards, an unseen pursuer throughout the race, the goddess of victory, Nike, swooped in for the *coup de grace.* Another Southern Californian, Kathleen McCartney, traipsed across the finish line first in 11:09:40. Moss needed another 29 seconds before she could drop a limp arm onto the finish stripe. The agony of Julie Moss and the ecstasy of Kathleen McCartney left an indelible impression on more than two million TV viewers, as powerful as that of Frank Shorter winning the 1972 Olympic marathon.

Little did Collins, or anyone else, realize that the triathlon would be a wunderkind. Its rise in popularity is without peer. Never has a sport attracted the attention of so many so quickly. Consider the numbers explosion at the Ironman: In 1978 and 1979, there were 15 crazies; in 1980 the total shot up to 100 fanatics; in 1981, when the course was moved to the Big Island, Hawaii, the number swelled to 350; in 1982, the February race attracted 590 serious athletes; the October '82 race reached its near-capacity of 850. More than 400 would-be contestants had to be turned away. This sport had made the boom in running sound more like a pop.

Triathlons elsewhere have witnessed equally fast growth. The first United States Triathlon Series (USTS) races (five of them at cities on the West Coast in 1982) sold out as soon as they were opened for applications. A hastily assembled publication by *Swim Swim* magazine, *Swim Bike Run,* listed 76 triathlons (a race consisting of a swim, bike ride and run) across the United States in 1982. Another 100 triathlons listed were actually multi-event races (any three sports combined into one race). There were, no doubt, another 50 triathlons that never made the list, thus bringing the nationwide total to more than 100 triathlons.

Amazingly, triathlon racing has spread to other continents — South America, Australia and Europe. At the October '82 Ironman, the Netherlands and Brazil fielded teams, and there were competitors from Australia, Saudi Arabia, Korea, Japan, New Zealand, Switzerland and England. In addition, International Management Group, the powerful representative of many world-class athletes, hosted an invitational triathlon in Nice, France.

IRONMAN: FATHER OF THE REVOLUTION

Leading the way of the triathloning movement has been the Ironman, father of the revolution. Ironman receives the most publicity; Ironman is the most difficult triathlon; Ironman is in beautiful Hawaii. Ironman's influence is so pervasive that other sponsors emulate the Ironman distance by calling their races "half-triathlons": The race distance is exactly half that of Hawaii's. And those who finish these less demanding triathlons are, in keeping with the challenge, called Tinmen. The Ironman, then, has become the yardstick by which all other races measure themselves.

The Ironman's army of 3000 volunteers gets its orders from a quiet, disarmingly beautiful blonde named Valerie Silk. She looks like anything but an Ironman. Silk took over the race after the 1980 edition, and has yet to stray from the path to success. She has guided and nurtured the Ironman through several organizational changes and a relocation, always staying one step ahead of chaos in this Cecil B. De Mille production.

Silk attributes the order to three crucial changes in the race organization since she assumed command: "I moved the course to a place that would be less congested [it was held on the busy roads around Oahu until 1981], I changed the date of the race from the winter to a fall date, and I eliminated the individual support ruling."

It is a tribute to Silk and the organization that the race has been free of life-threatening accidents to date. This is partly because a well-equipped medical staff attends to athletes on race day. As one doctor said, "On the day of the race, the participants will be the safest people on this island."

But the Ironman's popularity has also become its biggest liability. Silk says she will institute a strict qualifying standard, to cope with the number of triathletes wanting to enter. "This is such a tough event," she says, "that too many times we have people in the race who don't have any business being there at all." Just getting into the Ironman might soon be more difficult than completing it. Race officials have indicated that the absolute safe limit is about 1000 participants. Many more than 1000, however, want to compete.

Almost overnight, the Ironman became the holy grail for athletes because it offered a new challenge, it happened at the right time and in the right place, and it had glamour. But the Ironman went beyond stirring up interest in the triathlon; it sanctioned the combination of different sports into a single event, something previous multi-sport races had failed to accomplish. And it brought together one of the most diverse group of athletes imaginable, a group comprised of ex-professionals in baseball, football, basketball, tennis and golf; veteran endurance athletes, former Olympians and thrill seekers; captains of industry and your average, everyday athlete like you and me.

WHAT IS AN ATHLETE?

The root appeal of the triathlon might be grounded in the age-old barroom debate over who is an athlete and who makes the best athlete. This triple-threat sport, many argue, puts to rest any doubts about who is the best athlete.

The definition of an athlete varies from person to person, has a different meaning depending on which bar you visit, and depends to some extent on how many beers you had before you were asked the question. Is a bowler an athlete? A fisherman? A race car driver? A judo expert? A runner? A dancer? It depends on your definition. I define an athlete as anyone who participates in an event that requires the following: skill, endurance and strength. Those, however, who have skill but lack endurance or strength should be categorized as gamesmen or sportsmen. They are the bowlers, the fishermen, the hunters, the pool players, and so on. Would you call the famous pool player Minnesota Fats an athlete? I rest my case. Your beer-drinking, armchair athlete, of course, could counter your argument by knocking the runner. Running, he might say, requires about as much skill as toasting bread. "Anybody can put one foot in front of the other," he declares, slurring his words. But I doubt that anybody, not even the barroom gadfly, could argue that the triathlon isn't one of the most challenging endurance sports.

Who Is the Best Triathlete?

It's obvious — at least to triathletes — who is the best athlete, but what about the best triathlete? Is it the swimmer, the cyclist, or the runner? That remained a debatable question until the February 1982 Ironman awards ceremony. Winner Scott Tinley, upon accepting his award, settled the issue in so many words. "In 1980, Dave Scott, a swimmer, won the Ironman and concluded that swimmers make the best triathletes. In 1981, winner John Howard, a cyclist, declared that cyclists make the best triathletes. Now that I've won, and I'm a triathlete, I guess that proves that triathletes make the best triathletes."

Just to prove his point: In 1980, when Howard — a 1976 Olympian — entered the triathlon his first time, he proved to himself and to other athletes that the single-sport specialist has less chance of winning the Ironman than the well-rounded athlete In that race Scott, who had trained in all three events and keyed on the run and bike ride — his weakest sports — led Howard the entire distance even though Howard turned in a brilliant bike ride. Howard nearly drowned in the swim and was Kentucky-fried near the end of the marathon. When he returned to Hawaii the next year to win, he was much better trained, having spent the bulk of his time running and swimming.

Even the athlete who is strong in two events and weak in one is at a distinct disadvantage, as Scott Tinley, a mustachioed blonde from Southern California, found out in 1981. He was not much of a bike rider then. By 1982, he was explaining his victory in these brief words, "I learned how to ride a bike."

The world's best triathlete is probably about six years old now. His parents are triathletes and are teaching him how to ride a bicycle, to swim and to run. A decade from now we'll hear from him.

Ironmen on alloy bikes. Jeff (left) and Scott Tinley consistently finish among the top competitors at the Ironman. Here they ride the drops into a headwind at the October 1982 Ironman.

Triathlon On Stage

There is a host of reasons why the triathlon has been called by some the sport of the '80s. Among them: 1) It better defines the athlete. 2) It is a natural progression in endurance sports. 3) The training concept is holistic and synergistic. 4) The media has adopted it as three-ring entertainment. 5) It better accommodates training through injuries. 6) The popularity of cycling, running and swimming is at a new high. 7) A stable of endurance athletes has been waiting for a new challenge since the marathon came on the scene.

Tracing the evolution of sports in this country will put the triathlon's new-found popularity in perspective. Let's start with the sports participation explosion of 1919, the year the *New York Times* foresaw and reported on the burgeoning trend. One story read: "The nation, released from years of gloom and suppression, is expressing the reaction by plunging into sport "

In his book, *Sport — Mirror of American Life,* Robert H. Boyle writes that the sports boom came about from many different influences. "It is in large measure the end-product of a number of impersonal factors: industrialization, urbanization, increased leisure and income, commercial promotion and upper-class patronage." By the time of the Depression and the New Deal, Boyle writes, Americans began to participate more in sports because they had more free time. Thanks to the Industrial Revolution, providing for a family and putting food on the table was less of an ordeal. By the end of 1939, the average worker had one more day of leisure time than he had in 1929, and two days more than his counterpart in 1890.

But team sports were still the most popular activities among Americans in the early days and even all the way up to the early 1960s. The 1960s was the decade of revolutions — social, political, economic — and sport did not come out of the decade of change unscathed. James Michener discusses this in his book *Sports in America:* "The intellectuals' agitation of the 1960s, with their attack on all fronts against the establishment, made it inevitable that sports should be subjected to a more severe scrutiny, and the result was spectacular."

The result was that people evolved from passive participants to front-line weekend warriors. Doing was in and the health boom was under way, fueled in part by the birth of the Me Generation.

The health boom was further promoted by doctors and scientists who informed us that we had better clean up our acts or the body beautiful was going to become the body bankrupt. Their research showed that cigarette smoking was linked to lung cancer; obesity was suspected as a cause of high blood pressure and a variety of other ailments; lack of exercise was blamed for heart disease. Meanwhile, Dr. Kenneth Cooper's book, *Aerobics,* was published in 1968 and soon made the bestseller list, Jim Ryun set the world record in the mile in 1967 and President John F. Kennedy revitalized the President's Council on Physical Fitness.

While endurance sports were hardly front-page news back in the 1960s, any activity that glorified strength was the media rage, especially bodybuilding. Not that everyone was working out in gyms back then, but the heroes of many teen-agers were musclemen like Joe Weider, Charles Atlas, Jack LaLanne and, of course, Superman. Bodybuilding magazines had almost as much status as baseball cards. And the one personality trait that bodybuilders and weightlifters had in common with present-day endurance athletes was their individualism. A survey of weightlifters in the late 1940s bears this out. John B. Thune conducted his study at a YMCA in Oakland, California. According to Boyle, he revealed in a *Research Quarterly* article that weightlifters were shy and lacked self-confidence when compared to non-lifters at the YMCA. The weightlifter felt awkward playing most athletic games and often avoided the responsibility of leading others. He would, according to Thune, "find it a greater honor to win an individual championship than to be a member of a winning team."

The 1970s, however, were a different story. Strength was out; endurance was in. This was the decade of the runner. The sport became popular because it was relatively easy to do, required little time to maintain aerobic conditioning, and it involved a minor initial investment. There were no teams to join, either. A runner was a free spirit, which was important back in the early 1970s when doing your own thing was fashionable.

Runners were regarded initially as a bit strange. What kind of person enjoyed pounding the pavement? Aficionados of the sport, however, liked being called eccentric. For the most part, early runners were, by their own admission, eccentrics anyway. Take Bob Deines, for example. This top-notch marathoner wore his hair long, had a scraggly beard and was often seen running in a psychedelic-looking T-shirt.

Several other factors, however, made running the sport of the masses, such as Shorter's Olympic victory, Joe Henderson's poetic training prose advocating long, slow distance and *Runner's World* magazine's frequent articles on sane, humane training.

The 1970s were also kind to the other two sports of the triathlon. American swimmers won medals by the handfuls at the 1972 and 1976 Olympics. A bicycle boom, resulting from gas shortages and a general increasing health consciousness, culminated in the 1980 Academy Award-winning movie *"Breaking Away."* In the early 1970s the United States manufactured as many as 10 million bicycles in a single year, thus surpassing the total number of cars produced for a like period of time.

What of this decade? If the first two years are any indication, this will be the decade of the recreational athlete. You could jazz up the name a bit and call him the renaissance athlete. The triathlete, then, will be our Leonardo da Vinci. Being adept at more than one sport is in and, as Tinley aptly stated, "The triathlon is the ultimate expression of the Southern California lifestyle." Not cocaine.

The triathlon and other multi-event sports appear to fit right in with another unique California trend of the 1980s — holistic health. Holism, according to Webster's dictionary, is the view that an integrated whole has a reality independent of and greater than the sum of its parts. For example, when you enjoy a piece of pecan pie, you not only gain mental pleasure, but a pound or so of weight as well. When you think holistically, you think of the way events affect you both mentally and physically. The carry-over to the triathlon is a logical one. Triathlon training works all of the body's major muscles and the demands of the sports require a wide range of mental outlooks. Each sport strengthens the body and the mind.

The importance of cross-training (working out in two or more sports during a training program) is much greater than you might imagine. When combined, cycling, running and swimming become synergistic. That is, the sum of the parts is greater than the whole. Running will make you a better swimmer and cyclist; cycling will improve your running and swimming, and so on.

A FAD WITH A FUTURE?

By all indications, the triathlon is becoming a fad. By some estimates, the number of athletes who have entered triathlons since 1978 is only a little more than 100,000. Compare that to 30 million runners. The media are also scrambling for coverage of the sport. In 1982, CBS *"Sports Spectacular"* taped the Malibu Triathlon on a Saturday and aired it on Sunday. It was hardly an event on the scale of the Ironman but it received impressive coverage. And when Hollywood turns its attention to a sport, you know it must have some fad appeal. In 1982, Tinsel

Town announced that it was shopping for script writers to put together a made-for-TV movie using the Ironman as a backdrop.

But neither the glitter and pizzazz of Hollywood nor the broadcasting influence of the television networks is going to assure the future of the triathlon. It must rely on grass-roots support and behind-the-scenes sparkplugs like Jim Curl, Dave Standinger, Jim Gayton and Joe Oakes. Unfamiliar names to most people, these gentlemen are working for the triathlete in their efforts to establish a national governing body and put together safe, well-organized races.

USTA: Order Out of Chaos

In April 1982, at Sacramento, California, members of vying triathlon associations met to hammer out a plan for one national governing body, which resulted in the establishment of the United States Triathlon Association (USTA). Its first president, Jim Gayton, has a background in bike racing. Gayton, who resides in Southern California, reports that the first meeting was filled with political maneuvering as sponsors, race promoters and athletes jockeyed for power. To the surprise of many members the athletes prevailed and, as a result, the USTA by-laws included an inviolable condition that the board of directors consist of 80 percent active triathletes. In essence, the USTA is a political body of athletes, by athletes, for athletes, which Gayton notes is unique in amateur sports.

If you're an average triathlete, what happens with the USTA probably won't much concern you. But the top-ranked triathlete interested in making a living from the sport or who has Olympic aspirations depends on the success of the USTA, for unless the sport has a governing body, it cannot become an Olympic sport.

All of this is a moot point now for triathletes. There is no Olympic triathlon team. And an Olympic triathlon event will not be feasible until around the year 2000, assuming the sport continues to flourish worldwide.

Currently, the advantage of a national governing body for all triathletes is its power to pave the way in establishing a set of fair, realistic rules. It will bring order out of chaos. The USTA has already defined the triathlon — any event that combines swimming, cycling and running — and it is currently sanctioning races.

USTS: A Look at Things to Come

The United States Triathlon Series races were such a smash success in 1982 that the USTS expanded to 12 races, from coast to coast, in 1983. The series' creator, Carl Thomas, is a former All-American swimmer and current vice president of marketing for Speedo International. Its executor, Jim Curl, is a 33-year-old attorney who lives in Davis, California. His business as a full-time race promoter is called Endurance Sports Production.

With the creation of the USTS, Curl and Thomas established themselves overnight as leaders in triathlon promotion. Their races have set the pattern for the many triathlons that are sure to come. For example, the race distances of two-kilometer swim, 40-kilometer bike ride and 15-kilometer run have become standard. A good triathlete can finish in close to two hours, whereas an average triathlete's time might be closer to three hours, about the time it takes to run a marathon. The races are easy enough for a novice to train for without having to quit his job, get a divorce and sell his house.

The USTS races have, for the most part, received strong support from local clubs in the three sports of the triathlon. Fields have numbered between 400 and 1000, and the courses have been in out-of-the-way places — good for traffic control but bad for spectating. The triathlons are like other races in that they include the usual enticements common to running — T-shirts, a relay race, trophies, free beer, published race results and cash prizes. But the atmosphere at a triathlon is unique; it brings together athletes from every imaginable sport and allows them to share the same experience.

DRAFTING BECOMES AN ISSUE

At the October 1982 Ironman, the issue of drafting generated almost as much heat as the Big Island's active volcanoes. Accusations of drafting by some top finishers ruffled the feathers of many contestants, and one wonders if the bike ride wasn't really a bike race. On several occasions, race officials did warn triathletes that they were drafting. Apprised of the situation after the race, Valerie Silk sidestepped the problem to avoid "opening a Pandora's box." She would deal with drafting at the next Ironman. In general, triathletes are honest about obeying the drafting rule, but there are those who want stricter enforcement.

Drafting is the act of "sitting in" behind another cyclist's wheel to decrease wind drag and thus reduce energy expenditure. The procedure, which offers considerable advantage, is exactly like that used in car racing and, of course, bicycle racing. Chester Kyle, in a 1979 issue of *Ergonomics,* estimates the reduction in wind resistance at as much as 44 percent for the cyclist following at a distance of six inches. You can see, then, why drafting is not allowed. And even at a distance of eight feet, the advantage can be as much as 26 percent reduced wind resistance. Interestingly, Ironman rules require that a rider keep two bike lengths between himself and a lead rider, a distance at which there would still be a slight reduction in wind resistance.

The problem is that the bike portion of the triathlon is supposed to be the lone cyclist riding against himself and the clock. Because of the scarcity of entrants, the lone cyclist was not uncommon at the early Ironmans and other triathlons. But now, with hundreds of triathletes vying for the same strip of asphalt, avoiding the draft is nearly impossible. Riders almost have to work at *not* drafting other riders. Something as innocent as passing another rider can be construed as drafting.

Jim Curl says that he has grappled with the drafting debate for many hours. He has spoken with dozens of triathletes and race officials. He has reviewed the rules of time-trial racing in cycling and has talked with bike race officials to get their opinions. All of this input, he hopes, will lead to a rule that everyone can live by. The stakes are pretty high, too. "I realize," says Curl, "that all eyes are on the USTS and we want to come up with a set of rules that are equitable." He asserts that enforcing the drafting rule will ultimately be the burden of the meet director, not the athletes. "The athletes will complain and make their voices heard and probably influence the race directors in one way or another," states Curl, "but if the athletes really want one type of rule, they'll get it. Race directors are human. They don't want to piss off the athletes."

Curl says he gets a different suggestion on rules for drafting from each person he confers with. Everyone, it seems, has his own idea. It has even been suggested that there be no rule at all. Imagine the bike ride turning into a bike race! Although this would make for an interesting event, the chances of pileups would be much greater and experienced bike racers would have an obvious advantage.

Enforcement of the drafting rule could go the way of time-trial procedures used by the United States Cycling Federation (USCF). The USCF employs several officials who, on motorcycles, drive the course looking for offenders. Stationary judges, Curl emphasizes, don't work. As the judge sees a cyclist riding toward him, he has difficulty determining whether or not other riders nearby are drafting because there are only a few seconds to make a decision.

Once a triathlete is found guilty of drafting, what then? Do you disqualify him? Do you give him a time penalty? If it's a penalty, when do you enforce it? How long should it be? Do you enforce it when the race is over? Do you create a penalty box and hold him for a certain amount of time at the next transition area? The options are many. But based on the concern triathletes have expressed, an acceptable solution will probably result. Members of the sport would much rather get on with the race.

2

Metamorphosis

Once an athlete always an athlete — if not in body, then in spirit. Like most triathletes, I arrived at this sport through a metamorphosis, a gradual change of form from one kind of athlete to another. The changes were sometimes subtle, but always within the constraints of my personal goals and innate need to excel and compete physically. The metamorphosis I underwent to become a triathlete will be familiar to many involved with the sport. My reason for telling it is more to share my own positive attitude and chronicle the evolution of my training philosophy and strategy to what it is today. To be an athlete is a tenuous avocation: Each improvement in performance brings you closer to an absolute limit. Ultimately, age, injury, work and family will slow you down, but the spirit endures.

I have been an athlete in individual sports since the age of 12. Whether I recognized the psychological and sociological reasons for my lack of interest in team sports was irrelevant. I knew immediately that I sought and enjoyed both the freedom of working out alone, uncoached, and the discipline required to improve performance over time. Minimal facilities at a new school cut short an early gymnastics career for me. Without losing stride, however, I picked up a fiberglass pole and began vaulting, with moderate success, for a year. Because part of my training involved cross-country running, I decided to try distance running next. After only a few months I knew I had found my niche.

Throughout high school and college, I improved to the point where my primary identity was as a runner. Training, which provided as much or more enjoyment than racing, began to dictate lifestyle. Refining and defining, my mileage and intensity increased as I turned almost exclusively to marathoning. The better I ran, the more I ran. My self-employment as a painting contractor allowed me time during the day to train and during the winter season to race. I competed about 30 to 40 times a year; my emphasis was on quality, not quantity. The sport had become my medium for expression, much like a painter's artwork. The running boom was under way in the early 1970s when I was competing and I felt like a pioneer in a national movement. As my times in the marathon got lower, my goals got higher and the Olympic Trials marathon became my obsession.

My wave crest in running came on January 17, 1980, on a cold, foggy morning in Northern California — perfect race weather. It happened at the Paul Masson Marathon, the AAU National Championship race. I ran a 2:16:39, a career-best and good enough for fifth place (third American). I had qualified for the Olympic Trials a second time and had set my sights on a breakthrough performance for the Trials race in May. Ironically, on that January day I was washed up as a runner.

As the Olympic Trials drew near, it became clear that a nagging, apparently minor, hip injury, which had bothered me for two years already, was irrevocably and irreconcilably putting a stop to my plans. My 120-mile weeks became 80, 40 and then nothing. But rest didn't help, either. I spent thousands of dollars looking for a "miracle cure." Specialists — orthopedists, podiatrists, rolfers, acupuncturists — were unable to work any magic. Meanwhile, adding insult to injury, my obsession to continue running at all costs — it was my life and overtraining was my mistress — had overwhelmed any instincts to take a year or two off. As a result, I favored the hip injury for two years, long enough to develop osteoarthritis in my foot, which eventually became more debilitating than the original injury. I couldn't run more than 15 miles a week, yet here I was still in my prime, not having reached my full potential, forced to sit on the shore as my wave crashed on the beach. I felt like an athlete dying on the vine. Little did I realize at that moment that the process of metamorphosis was taking place inside me.

Like all athletes, I faced a turning point once again. Retire? Continue running at a less competitive level, or undergo metamorphosis once again? The choice was not immediately obvious. Because running had involved such a commitment, I was less objective and very bitter. I hadn't yet received from running what I had expected. I was disgusted with myself, disillusioned with the medical profession, although I knew that overtraining and overzealousness was at the root of it all. This time the process of change was painful.

Before I gave up running completely, I decided to lay off temporarily. Out of frustration and fear of getting fat, I started cycling to keep aerobically fit. After three weeks, I was ready to throw the bike back into the garage. My endurance was still at a very high level, but my legs were unused to their new pursuit and would tie up even when I was hardly breathing. Luckily, I met some local cyclists who were willing to pull me along on a ride one Sunday. I recruited my competitive juices to keep from humiliating myself that day and I saw the light — the potential for improvement in a new sport with new goals and challenges.

Not long after the introduction to cycling in 1980, I started riding with Ian Jackson. He, too, had been a runner before turning to cycling and now he was planning to enter the Ironman. Aware that I was depressed over my running predicament, he decided to challenge me in the triathlon. I knew nothing of the Ironman, but the metamorphosis was under way and there was no turning back.

THE EVOLUTION OF A TRIATHLETE

The decision to become a triathlete begins a long process of evolution. A case of survival of the fittest, it is an experiment of one, full of constant adaptations to survive the triathlon, the training and the racing In 1980, there was no published information on how to train for the triathlon. Cross-training had been coined as a training term only in the past year. It was a case of the blind leading the blind.

I knew I would have to spend a lot more time training than I ever had as a runner (100 miles a week is only about 11 hours worth of work), but I was more than ready to put in extra time cycling and swimming to take my mind off my abandoned running career. It was early in September 1980 when I began to train seriously for the February 1981 Ironman. My cycling immediately climbed to more than 300 miles a week. Several times a week I would jump into a pool and flail about, uncoached, for 5000 meters without rest. The effect, as planned, was disorientation and sickness, all in an effort to simulate ocean conditions. Because of my injury, I could run only 15 to 20 miles a week, but at a relatively fast pace with my foot taped up to the middle of my calf. I had no diary or log. I just made it up as I went along. Because I was also working full time as a painting contractor, I was always tired, and my social life deteriorated as weekends became two-day opportunities to overtrain.

Then the colds started. By November I had been running on the red line too long – my overtraining had lead to sickness. From November to January, I had four lingering colds, the last just two weeks before the Ironman. The stress of working and overtraining in the cold, wet, Northern California winter was too much. I tried desperately to back out, to get my entry fee back. Ian Jackson convinced me otherwise, however, and I decided to go through with it – to have an enjoyable time and just finish.

I'll never regret my decision. The Ironman was not the drudgery I had feared. Instead, I was overwhelmed by its complexity, by the prerace energy. And the camaraderie during and after the race made a triathlete out of me. My accomplishment in the race simply enticed me to return to improve on a 24th-place finish. I knew I had made several errors in training and tactics: 1) I had overrated my swimming and cycling abilities or, at least, had trained improperly in those sports. 2) I had overtrained in general. 3) Remembering the dangers of dehydration from my running days, I went overboard drinking fluids (30 to 35 pints) during the race; consequently, I spent a lot of time off the bike correcting my mistake. 4) By not applying a lubricant before the race, I suffered severe chafing in the swim. 5) By the time I got to the run, my legs were shot from too much spinning. 6) I went out too fast in the run, which is how I had trained, and thus had to walk a lot during the marathon. 6) My attitude prior to the race had been far too negative as a result of my overtraining.

Rather than being a swan song, however, the race had given me a new focus for competitive drive. I vowed to return and do myself justice next time, a common feeling among triathletes. Suddenly I realized that I was a triathlete and that running by itself would never have the meaning it had had for me. With renewed enthusiasm, I analyzed my training and the programs of others. It was clear to me that I could do well in this sport if I could avoid breaking down in training, and if I concentrated more on technique.

I returned to California and began an experimental period, resting completely for six weeks after the Ironman before resuming training. After the rest, I did only maintenance-type training eight hours a week, consisting mostly of cycling. In May I set my goals for February 1982 to break 10 hours and place in the top 10, even though I was working 40 hours a week and wanted to work until the final phase of my training. I wanted to control my training program, not vice versa. So after work, instead of 50 or 60 miles at an easy pace, I rode hard 15 to 20 miles, swam rarely and ran only after riding. Training amounted to one or two hours three days a week and 10 hours total on the weekends. For some reason, I was becoming stronger.

In the fall of 1981, I entered two half-triathlons, thinking that they would be a good measure of my condition and the effectiveness of my experiment. At the Sierra Nevada Triathlon in September, I nearly drowned in the swim, which was the first indication that I needed some work on both technique and ability to judge direction in the water, not to mention my skill in dealing with schools of thrashing swimmers. By the time I got out of the water, I was 225th. I had intended to ride the bike as hard as I could that day to see whether I could then survive the run.

I rode well on the bike. For the first time, I felt like a strong cyclist. I moved up 200 places in the 56-mile ride and continued to gain ground in the run in a survival shuffle, finishing fourth overall.

For the Santa Barbara Triathlon in October, I planned to swim, ride and run as hard as I could to test my limitations. Better to drop out of the Santa Barbara Triathlon than enter Hawaii with false hopes and faulty training methods. That rainy day in Santa Barbara introduced me to hypothermia, and to the winner of the February 1982 Ironman — Scott Tinley. I was lucky that the swim was only one mile; the water temperature of 61 degrees left me shivering uncontrollably 20 miles into the bike ride. I swam much better this time — my work on technique was paying off — and rode well over the hilly course as hard as I had planned. The run, despite my injuries and lack of training, proved to be the most encouraging sign that day. My 1:15 half-marathon pushed me up to second place, only six minutes behind Tinley. I had proved to myself that it was possible to go a lot harder in both racing and training as long as a smart pace is maintained and the body has been trained to deal with all possibilities. Improvements in performance are almost inevitable.

I now knew exactly what to expect from my body in Hawaii if I stuck with the plan. I set about doing those workouts that would bring the greatest return for the least amount of down-time and wear and tear. In swimming, that meant working initially on technique, which is so much more significant than strength. I got a coach to evaluate my form. As it improved, I began doing work with hand paddles and pull buoys — always quality work. This allowed me to cut my swimming yardage in half, to less than 5000 yards a week.

On the bike I rode as hard as I could — no garbage mileage.

If I couldn't average at least 21 mph on the bike (my intended pace for the Ironman) for my rides of less than 75 miles, I would turn around and go home. That was my gauge of recovery. Some people take their pulse in the morning; I just go out and see how I feel. Within five miles, I know whether to continue or give it up. My total mileage decreased as my intensity increased. With better rest and more of it, I found myself getting stronger.

I decided I needed to do some combination workouts. I set a goal of doing 10 rides in excess of 100 miles, followed by a run of any length, over a four-month period. The least I ran after these rides was three miles, the most was 11. I did three of the combination workouts without eating, and they were all hard rides over hilly terrain in 5:30 or less. My goal was to bonk purposely in the ride. I wanted to duplicate race conditions as closely as possible and I wanted to feel rotten for the run. I discovered to my pleasure and amazement, however, that I could get off the bike feeling lousy and still feel good in the run. I noticed a difference in my ability to burn fats and I began to feel stronger at five hours than I had at four. I also discovered that some glycogen remains in the leg muscles because of the use of different muscles in cycling and running.

It was all coming together — 175 miles a week on the bike, 20 to 25 miles a week running (I would have done more if my injuries had allowed) and 5000 yards a week swimming was yielding more benefits than mileage twice that total the previous year. Three long, hard workouts a week provided the backbone; shorter workouts and rest filled the gaps. My health and resistance to illness increased as a result, and because I began to supplement my diet with larger doses of vitamins.

The strategy rewarded me with a near-perfect peak the day of the February 1982 Ironman. I was well-rested from my taper and chomping at the bit. Everything went as hoped. The swim took a little longer, but the bike ride was great. I didn't overhydrate this time, and I ate well and rode as hard as I could under the conditions. I settled into a slightly slower pace in the run, which I knew by now I could sustain over most of the course. The result — 92nd out of the water, 10th on the bike and fourth overall at 9:57:14 — was well under both goals. I was the first finisher who was not a full-time triathlete.

I learned this much about myself from the whole experience: There is never any reason to give up. I had thought my athletic career doomed after I was injured when actually, a new and wider realm of possibilities was opened up to me. Ah, metamorphosis!

3

Float, Coast and Shuffle

SWIMMING

If you can't swim, you've got your work cut out for you. Swimming is a big stumbling block for many runners and cyclists intent on entering the triple-fitness sport. If you can't run, that isn't so bad; you can jog, you can walk, you can even crawl. If you can't cycle, you can at least coast. How many people do you know who can't ride a bike? But what happens if you can't swim? You drown. A lousy runner or cyclist who can swim well will finish a triathlon; a poor swimmer could be fished from the water. Your ability to swim one mile, or even the length of a pool, depends not on how strong you are or what kind of swimming trunks you wear, but on technique.

Learned to swim as a kid you say? You've got a head start on everyone else. If you are over 20 and can't swim, there is still hope. But you'll need the zeal of a religious fanatic to succeed. It might be several months before you can swim the length of a pool, or even tread water. I've heard one excuse from many athletes, however, that doesn't hold water. They claim that they sink like a rock. But body fat is not essential to be a good swimmer; just ask Mark Allen. The Southern California lifeguard emerged from the ocean seconds behind Dave Scott at the October 1982 Ironman and he's got about 5 percent body fat. When I'm in top shape, I don't even have to blow all the air out of my lungs to sink to the bottom of the pool.

Triathlon rules are strict about the swim — no flotation devices or other gear to assist your forward momentum. So if you intend to enter a triathlon, you had better be sure before the starting gun sounds that you can swim the distance, which is usually about one mile.

I was fortunate; I knew how to swim before I decided to enter the Ironman. But as a pool swimmer, I had no experience in open-water swimming, which, as you might guess, is somewhat more difficult. When I arrived in Hawaii, I learned the hard way on my first ocean swim. I worked out with some friends who were experienced ocean swimmers. About a half-mile from the beach, the swells got so high that I couldn't see the shore. I got scared, and I don't scare easily. I turned around and headed back to the security of Kailua Pier. By race time a week later, praise be to Neptune, I was a seasoned ocean swimmer and had no problem completing the 2.4 miles. It's not unusual for contestants in Hawaii to be swimming in the ocean for the first time. One of those swimmers said she was so scared that for the entire distance, she never looked down in the water.

Swimmers Aren't All Wet

If you can't swim a stroke you should spend several months becoming accustomed to water before even thinking about a one-mile open-water swim. First, get a coach; then join a masters swim program. A masters organization usually has its own coach on staff. Swimming pools are few and far between, accomplished swim coaches diamonds in the rough. But by joining a masters program (see Appendix for the national governing body to contact), you gain access to a pool and meet other swimmers as well.

Why is a coach so essential? Because swimming, unlike other sports, requires someone to watch your technique and point out mistakes. It's difficult for you to judge how good your stroke and kick are. The unique buoyancy properties of water lead to sensory deprivation.

Many triathletes have a tendency to key on their best event and practice only occasionally at their weak ones. They train just enough to get by. The mediocre swimmer, however, might find himself struggling in the ocean. Contestants have been swept into the rocky Kona shoreline during the Ironman for lack of strength and experience

STROKE BY STROKE

Although I consider myself a competent swimmer, I hired a coach after the 1981 Ironman. At the following year's event, I took several minutes off my swim time. Another good training aid for swimming is the videotape machine. You can film your swimming style and analyze it with your coach. And, as is true with any sport, the more time you spend practicing, the better you'll be. How do you think fish got to be such great swimmers?

I offer some pointers on swimming here, but only as they apply to the triathlon.

Stroke: Almost without exception, triathletes use the crawl or free-style stroke in competition. The exception is the champion breast-stroke swimmer who can swim faster and more efficiently using that stroke Then there was the little old Japanese man in the 1981 Ironman who swam the entire distance on his back. He hung a mirror around his neck and held it up once in a while to see where he was going. He finished last, but he wasn't in any hurry.

You might consider changing strokes to get your bearings; you can often see better using a side, breast or back stroke. The best strategy is to draft another swimmer and follow his kick to avoid spending time and energy looking around. If that strategy doesn't work for you, then look up and ahead every eight to 10 strokes. Pick out the tallest or most obvious landmark near your goal and swim for it Ocean swells make your task more difficult, both for swimming and for sighting, so it's helpful to time your sighting for the moment you crest the swell. In the trough, all you'll get is a face full of water.

Taking the Plunge: The swim is usually the first event in triathlon competition, although occasionally it is saved for last, which I consider a hazard. Should the swim come first, you can take several steps to prepare yourself: 1) Apply Vaseline to your armpits and thighs. The skin in these sensitive areas is susceptible to chafing, especially in saltwater. 2) Get your goggles ready by summoning up some old-fashioned spit to lubricate the insides of the lenses. The coating of saliva reduces the chance of the lenses fogging. Don't forget to rinse the goggles afterward. There are also several good commercial anti-fog agents available. 3) Check out the course so that you'll know the exact location of the buoys you'll swim around. 4) Before the race starts, go for a brief warm-up swim to avoid the shock of entering the usually cold water. If the water is very cold, wear a heavy rubber cap; it will reduce heat loss through the head. 5) Seed yourself. The charge from shore is fast and furious. If you're not properly positioned, you'll get trampled, or step on someone yourself.

The dash to water at the 1982 Monterey Triathlon was fast and furious. Be sure to seed yourself.

Hypothermia: Although most triathlons are held during the summer months to take advantage of warmer water, the danger of hypothermia is always a threat, even when the water temperature is a balmy 80 degrees. Diana Nyad can vouch for that. She suffered near-hypothermia during her failed attempt to swim from Cuba to Florida, even though the water was a constant 75 degrees. The body must expend energy not only to propel itself, but to maintain its 98.6-degree core temperature as well. Once fatigue sets in, hypothermia soon follows. Hypothermia becomes more of a threat as the water temperature drops, and body fat doesn't prevent the shakes. Dave Horning, three-time winner of the Escape From Alcatraz Triathlon, weighs a hefty 190 pounds, but he's well-aware of the threat of hypothermia. On one seven-mile swim in the chilly San

Francisco Bay, his entire right arm was numbed by the cold.

There are other hazards lurking in the water, like seaweed, Portuguese Man of War jellyfish, stinging sea nettles, speed boats and, need I remind you, sharks. Chances of falling victim to any one of these are slim, but still within the realm of possibility. At one Ironman, a top female competitor, Shawn Wilson, stepped on a sea nettle a few days prior to the race, and the swelling and pain that resulted forced her to withdraw. Another sea creature, the Man of War, has a dreadful reputation and demeanor, but its stings pose no threat unless you happen to be allergic to the toxin—or get stung in the eye. As for sharks, pray that they aren't hungry, and get out of the water if you see any. If you're bleeding, get out of the water even quicker; you're ringing the shark's dinner bell. Horning cut himself on a reef before the Maui Cross-Channel Swim in 1982 and, with blood oozing down his side, he got out of the water immediately. Everyone who saw him panicked and yelled, "Oh, oh! Shark bait!" Horning wiped off the blood, shrugged and started his swim. The sharks looked the other way.

Training for Open-Water Swimming

Before a triathlon, practice swimming in open water, preferably over the course you'll race. If the race includes an ocean swim, go for an ocean swim. Do what you must to avoid the shock of entering a race in unfamiliar waters. You never know how your body will react in cold water until you've tried swimming in it.

Play it safe and swim where there is a lifeguard station, swim with a friend or have someone follow in a boat. Whatever you do, don't swim alone. If you're a novice open-water swimmer, start by swimming close to shore and then work your way out as you gain confidence.

Fins and Gills

Numerous training aids are available to the swimmer. Unfortunately, no one has yet devised a set of gills. Most of the training aids mentioned here cost between $4 and $12, so they're not going to soak you for your life fortune. The small investment, however, will yield hefty dividends. The training aids are not intended as crutches for the beginner; rather, they are meant to improve technique and build strength.

Kickboard: Kickboards are made of styrofoam, and are about two feet long and a foot wide. They're invaluable for practicing your kick. Extend your arms in front of you, grasp the edges of the board and kick. Lower your head into the water to increase

The paraphernalia of running and swimming. 1) Hand paddles 2) Vaseline 3) Speedo goggles 4) Kickboard 5) Pull buoys 6) Swim trunks 7) Rubber swim cap 8) Nylon running shorts 9) Cotton mesh singlet 10) Converse running shoes.

speed. Beginners might find the head-down position essential for maintaining forward momentum. You can also hold the kickboard behind your head and practice kicking while on your back.

Pull Buoy: A pull buoy usually consists of two pieces of styrofoam connected by nylon cloth. It fits between your thighs, thus keeping your legs horizontal in the water without having to kick and allowing you to concentrate on your stroke. Pull buoys also aid in the development of a sense of streamline and body rotation.

Fins: Fins look like duck feet and allow you to derive the same benefit that a duck does from its feet. They help improve kick efficiency and assist in strength training.

Inner Tube: I use a resistance-training program with a bicycle inner tube. Attach one end of the tube to the edge of the pool; attach the other end to a belt around your waist. Swim away from the edge until the inner tube is stretched taut; at that point, when resistance is greatest, swim hard enough to maintain your position.

Goggles: Goggles are clear plastic lenses that fit over your eyes. If you must wear eye glasses, prescription goggles are available, or you could take a chance and wear contacts. Goggles may look weird on you, but they improve visibility 100 percent and keep your eyes from being burned out by chlorine and salt water. Most goggles leak a little, even the most expensive brands. Find the pair that best conforms to your face and leaks the least. Dave Horning is unique among triathletes in his preference for the full-size face mask. He claims it provides better visibility than goggles and keeps out the water. Goggles are sold with clear or tinted lenses.

Hand Paddles: Hand paddles accentuate incorrect stroke movement. They slip over the palms of the hands and are held by elastic straps. The paddle, a sheet of plastic about four to six inches square, increases muscle recruitment with each stroke. Paddles are used to improve technique and build the arm and chest muscles.

BICYCLING

In training for a triathlon, I prefer bicycling to swimming and running. It's a good thing, too, because cycling consumes the majority of the triathlete's training hours and the bicycle portion of the race also takes the most time. So if you don't like cycling, consider not entering the triathlon — or take up

Chinese checkers. Cycling demands more in almost every respect, including your hard-earned money. If you don't own a good bike, plan on forking over at least four C-notes to your friendly bike shop. You should also invest in some cycle clothing and spare parts, which could total another three C-notes. By this time, you're probably thinking more seriously about Chinese checkers. Take heart, though: At least there aren't any pool fees.

Tech Talk

We know good technique is a matter of life and death in swimming. A mere notch down on the save-your-hide scale, is cycling technique, a good one of which is essential for top performance. I don't judge a cyclist by the kind of bike he rides, or by how many gears he has, but by the trueness of his line (and the number of calluses on his hands).

A veteran bike racer set me straight on how to become a better cyclist. "It's a matter of time on the bike," he said, as we set off on a 100-miler. After many such rides, I knew he was right. Spending six hours on a bike seat in one workout won't do wonders for your rear end, but it will make you a better cyclist, and you'll see a lot of beautiful countryside on backwoods roads, too. Nothing beats experience — finding the correct line through corners or the natural body sway that comes with getting off the saddle and climbing hills. Eventually, execution and split-second timing become second nature.

More so than swimming and running, cycling is a head game, a game in which confidence makes or breaks the rider. Don't let fear of falling limit your ability to make the right moves. Accidents are infrequent, usually minor, and mostly the result of rider error.

Riding a Straight Line

Before you start taking corners as though you were sitting atop a high-speed motorcycle, learn three things: how to ride in a straight line, hold the handlebars properly and shift gears. Sounds easy, but even some experienced cyclists can't manage these fundamental tasks.

First, steering. As his body weight shifts on the saddle while he pedals, the novice cyclist will sometimes oversteer to maintain a straight line. The situation is worsened by a seat that is too high. Practice riding in a straight line to correct this habit. For a warmdown following a ride, find a vacant lot that has a long, straight painted stripe to follow. Keep both wheels within three inches of the stripe as you pedal.

Second, holding the bars. Grip the handlebars firmly: The rougher the road surface, the tighter the grip. Think of your arms as shock absorbers for the bumps in the road. If you keep your arms ramrod straight, you'll take more of a pounding and have less control. When braking hard, however, brace your arms; otherwise you'll lunge forward and lose control. The bars are held more for control, steering and balance than for bearing your weight.

Third, shifting gears. Reaching to shift gears temporarily lessens your control over the bike. Most shift levers are on the down tube, so you have to extend a hand to use them. Avoid shifting gears in situations where both hands are needed for steering, such as on a bumpy road or when banking into a corner.

Gears allow you to maintain a steady cadence over uneven terrain. One gear doesn't make you go faster than another, but by using bigger gears, you can apply more torque to the pedals. Your strength determines your speed. Many cyclists make the common mistake of shifting gears when they are pedaling too slowly. The chain doesn't move easily from one freewheel cog to another (or one chainwheel to another) or won't shift at all. When there is too much tension on the chain and your rpm is low, the chain shifts with difficulty. You should shift before you are in a position (usually on a steep hill) that puts extra tension on the chain.

Cornering

Choose your line of travel through a corner before you enter the corner. Once you start the turn you won't have time to make changes in speed, lean, direction or body position. Riding on tortuous mountain roads is not a requirement for gaining expertise at cornering, but it does help. You can practice cornering just by riding around your neighborhood. Here is the four-step procedure for taking a corner:

1) **Getting Set.** Apply your brakes before banking into a turn. The speed at which you take a corner depends on many factors: road conditions (water, gravel, oil, rocks), tightness of the turn, its banking, cycling experience, type of tires you're riding on and your line going into the turn. Consider these factors as you set up for the turn. They will determine your speed, line and degree of braking once you position yourself for the turn.

Unless you're an experienced cyclist, do not pedal through the corner or turn; a pedal can easily catch on the road and make you lose control. With experience, however, you will find that pedaling through corners can be done safely.

Enter the curve from as far out in the road as possible, but do not ride into the lane of oncoming traffic unless you know the road is closed or you can see around the corner.

2) Choosing a Line. Your line should form a smooth arc from beginning to finish. The middle of your arc comes closest to the sharpest section of the hairpin corner. Otherwise, on a gradual curve, the arc is equidistant from the inside of the curve throughout. A sudden change in steering, body position or braking can result in a loss of control. To avoid losing control, you should be positioned properly before banking into the curve.

Once you've banked into the curve, look ahead at the road and through the curve, about 10 to 15 feet. Let your eyes follow your imaginary line and guide your bike through the curve. When riding, always survey the road ahead to pick out potential hazards.

3) Body Position. In keeping with the laws of physics (centrifugal force), the bike will lean into the curve, and you with it. The degree of lean depends on speed, road conditions, tightness of the curve and its banking. The higher your speed, the more you lean. Remember to keep the pedal facing the inside curve up to avoid scraping it on the road.

Usually a cyclist will corner while keeping up the knee facing the inside curve. There is an alternative to this method, however, which is especially valuable when taking corners on a bumpy road. Keeping both pedals parallel to the ground, take most of your weight off the saddle and put it into your legs. Think of your legs as similar to the shock absorbers on a car. Your legs reduce your unsprung weight — that weight unsupported by a spring suspension — by supporting your body weight. The *more* unsprung weight you have, the longer your wheels remain off the ground after hitting bumps in the road. With your body weight in your legs (the shocks), the wheels will be off the ground for less time because there is less unsprung weight. Increased control and traction will thus result. The principle is the same as that for a car with independent suspension. Its only unsprung weight is the wheels themselves. The less time the wheels are off the ground, the more control you have.

4) Recovery. Once past the tightest part of the turn (where your lean will be greatest), and as the road straightens, lean upright. Get set for the next turn.

The traditional method of cornering is to keep up the knee facing the inside curve. Note position of hands on drops for maximum control.

By keeping the pedals parallel to the ground while cornering, the rider can place weight onto his legs. Taking weight off the seat decreases a rider's unsprung weight.

Riding Position

I want to expose another myth about cycling regarding riding position on the 10-speed: You don't always ride with your hands on the bottom of the bars (drops). Bike racers only ride the drops about half the time, even when competing. You ride in this tucked position, not for increased comfort, but to reduce wind resistance. Although wind resistance is a major force that slows you down, riding while tucked is the least comfortable position, and it can cause back pain after a long ride.

Because you have better control and braking ability in this position, tuck when descending or when riding into a headwind — even during a workout. In a short race with a 15-mile bike ride or less, the tuck is more important. In longer triathlons, however, comfort is the overriding concern. Don't forget that you still have to run.

Hand Position

There are numerous places for your hands on the bars, but when you change your position, do so only when maintaining full control is not essential. Placing the hands equidistant from the center of the stem, where it holds the bars, will facilitate handling and control. For casual riding, I usually ride with my hands on the top, straight part of the bars. In situations when I might have to brake quickly, I will ride with my hands gripping the tops of the brake-lever posts. I can then apply the brakes with my fingers and still grasp the tops of the posts. But when control and instant braking are necessary, I ride the drops with my hands directly behind the brake-lever posts, two fingers from each hand resting on the brake levers. This is the position at which brake leverage is greatest.

Saddle Height: Saddle height can affect performance dramatically, so much so that a difference of a few millimeters will reduce efficiency. And a seat that is at the incorrect height can increase the chance of knee injury.

Eddy Merckx, five-time winner of the Tour de France, was obsessed with seat height. He would pull out his allen wrench and make seat adjustments in the heat of competition — while riding — to get that extra 1 percent advantage from his pedal stroke. You probably won't care to risk a seat adjustment while riding, so here is an easy way to determine acceptable seat height when stationary. All you need to adjust is your seat post.

Sitting on the bike in your normal position, hands on the bars, place your feet in the pedals (wearing your regular cycling

Placing hands on the straight portion of the handlebars offers the most in comfort, the least in control.

Placing hands over the brake lever posts is a good position for quick braking.

Ride with your hands on the drops for maximum control and maximum braking power.

shoes). There should be a slight bend in the knee at the point of greatest extension. Too much bend and the seat is too low; no bend and the seat is too high.

The seat itself can be adjusted in two directions on the seat post — forward and backward, and up and down. These are the finer position adjustments in cycling, but basic guidelines are as follows: Up and down: The seat should be horizontal to the ground or tipped up a few degrees. Forward and backward: The middle of the saddle is bisected by the extended central axis of the seat post. If you find that you constantly have to push back on the saddle to get comfortable or else scrunch forward, your seat is probably not in the proper position for you.

There is one more important adjustment to make on your bike to increase comfort and efficiency — stem length. Stems are sold in different lengths because people come in different shapes and sizes. Some have short torsos, some have long torsos, others have short arms or long arms. Here is one way to determine "proper" stem length: Sit on the saddle and assume your normal riding position. If you feel stretched out in an uncomfortable position, the stem is too long. If you feel crowded, it's too short. These sensations are more readily apparent after a

To find proper seat height, extend one leg as far as it will go. Your knee should be slightly bent.

long ride. Many cyclists cite hocus-pocus rules of thumb, such as sighting down at your front hub to see if your handlebars obscure it, but the final judgment on correct adjustments is *comfort.*

Rider position here is not too cramped or too stretched out. Stems come in different sizes to accommodate the rider.

UPS AND DOWNS IN CYCLING

Before discussing technique in climbing and descending, I want to prove a point: A good climber who is only a fair descender has an advantage over a fair climber who is a good descender. Descending skills should be learned more for reasons of safety than for saving time in the triathlon. The following scenario will demonstrate what I mean: A fair climber/good descender and good climber/fair descender begin an ascent of one mile together. The good climber pulls away, knowing that in order to stay ahead, he must maintain a strong pace and drop his opponent, or he will be passed on the descent. The good climber averages 15 mph on the gradual climb and thus takes four minutes; meanwhile, the good descender takes five minutes, averaging only 12 mph. So far, the good climber has a one-minute lead. The average descender manages 30 mph and takes two minutes for the one-mile descent, while the good descender needs only 1.5 minutes and averages 40 mph. But after the climb and descent, the good climber is still 30 seconds ahead.

The good descender made up only half the time he lost on the ascent. One-mile hills are found primarily in hilly terrain, but in a race over rolling hills, the amount of climbing adds up.

A sure way to become a good climber is to lose weight. You could also move to the Rocky Mountains to train, or simply work on technique. Some cyclists argue that good climbers are born, not made. They cite the pro cyclists from flatland countries, like Belgium and Denmark, who never train in the mountains yet are with the leaders during races in the Alps.

Back to technique. On particularly steep hills, or when you just want a change of pace, stand on the pedals; get out of the seat and place more of your weight on your hands as they grasp the brake-lever posts. Getting out of the saddle and pedaling will increase your leverage as you place more body weight over

Dave Scott gets out of the saddle momentarily during the October 1982 Ironman to stretch and power his way up a gradual incline.

The author, Mark Sisson, climbing while seated. Note position of his hands.

the pedals. There is considerable debate, however, over which is more efficient while climbing — standing up or sitting down. I have seen great climbers do both. For maximum effort, cyclists generally get out of the saddle, but on long, gradual climbs, pedal cadence is usually easier to maintain by sitting in the saddle and grinding it out, and only occasionally standing up to use different muscles.

It is not unusual for the frame to weave from side to side slightly as you work up the hill, although the wheels should follow a straight line. To practice on flat ground, shift into your biggest (hardest) gear. Now get out of the saddle and pedal. Learn to "flow" with the bike as it weaves from side to side; don't resist this natural motion. Your hands should grasp the tops of the brake-lever posts.

With practice, you will get used to getting out of the saddle. Standing up is especially beneficial for me because of my running experience. I found that standing up uses more of the muscles used in running. Ultimately, the best way to climb a hill is to do what is most comfortable for you. For most, that means a combination of sitting and getting out of the saddle.

When you do sit, sit as far back on the saddle as you can without sacrificing comfort. This position allows for a longer leg stroke and hence more leverage.

If you get out of the saddle to climb, your bike sways back and forth with each pedal stroke.

Note that the wheels are in a straight line.

Some Triathletes' Cranks Are Longer Than Others

A more radical way to increase leverage is to use longer crank arms. Standard-length crank arms on 10-speeds are 170 millimeters, but it's possible to obtain crank arms as long as 185 millimeters (170, 172.5, 175, 180, 185 are the options). Generally, a five-millimeter step-up will provide sufficient increase in leverage without reducing your rpm significantly.

Pushing Big Gears on Hills

Most triathletes don't like hills. The idea is to climb them as fast as possible. The bigger the gear you can push, the faster you'll go. Of course, you have to maintain a cadence of about 40 to 50 rpm; less and you begin to weave too much. You may have been told by bike racers that spinning a small gear at a quicker cadence will get you up a hill faster, but it won't. It takes power to climb a hill. Use your low gears (easy gears) for the steepest grades. An experienced athlete with several months of cycling behind him should practice pushing bigger gears.

My change from pushing low gears at high rpm to bigger gears at less rpm has been evolutionary, and many triathletes who get into cycling have said likewise. I used to climb hills around the Santa Cruz Mountains of Northern California in a 42 - 28. but now it's more like a 42 - 17.

A Decent Descent

There is really no reason to descend like some wild-eyed madman, unless you're a competent descender and willing to take the risks. Your speed should be based on experience, not on an attempt to make up time on a rider ahead of you. Remember that you're not a bike racer who needs to stay with the pack for drafting purposes. You are a triathlete who still has a run ahead of him, so ride with safety in mind.

During a descent, the tuck position is most practical because it reduces wind resistance and puts you in full control of your brake levers. On some descents in the Rocky Mountains and the Sierra Nevada, reaching speeds of 65 mph is not unusual. On these long straightaways, give your brakes a reassuring tap to slow down. To further reduce speed, sit up in the saddle to increase wind resistance.

A drawback about being a novice cyclist and riding with experienced bike racers is that they are invariably better descenders. The neophyte has a tendency to take more risks in an effort to stay with better riders. The racers sometimes further exacerbate the situation by needling the neophyte at the bottom of the hill. If you just take this good-natured ribbing in stride, you will be able to learn a lot from them about descending. Descending is an art, and as with any artistic endeavor, it improves with time. I usually tell them, in jest, that I had to stop to change a flat.

THE BICYCLE: $100 A POUND, AND MORE

Although it is the triathlete's most expensive investment, a bike will last a lifetime. Contrary to the popular myth, a bike frame does not lose structural integrity with age.

What bike is right for you? That depends on the seriousness of your intentions. I've seen people enter the Ironman on $100 "throwaways": When a part breaks, they throw away the entire bike. If you're a serious triathlete willing to invest some money, buy a quality 10-speed (a generic term that describes any bike with a derailleur, and with anywhere from five to 21 gears). There are several advantages to buying a quality 10-speed: 1) fewer mechanical breakdowns, 2) more efficiency, 3) spare part availability, 4) significant weight savings, and 5) more responsive handling.

The guide to quality is price. There is little difference among manufacturers, by nation or brand. Prices for a new, quality 10-speed start at $400. A bike for this price will get the job done, and then some. The next monetary bracket is in the neighborhood of $600 to $800. Bikes in this price range are usually made of lighter, double-butted tubing and higher-quality components. The most expensive bikes, which are $800 and up (about $100 per pound because they weigh about 20 pounds), offer the most advanced tubing, handcrafted workmanship and excellent components.

Which bike is best for you? First, check your pocketbook. Then ask yourself how ambitious you are. How much do you enjoy cycling? How good are you at fixing things? How big is your ego? Is it bigger than your pocketbook? If so, you're in trouble. The differences in performance between a $400 bike and a $1000 bike are not as much as many cyclists like to believe.

Purchase the new bike from a reputable bicycle shop, preferably one that has a qualified mechanic and several lines of popular bike brands to choose from. With any mechanical ability at all, you can learn to overhaul your bike. I recommend you do your own work. If you know basic maintenance procedures, you'll find potential mechanical problems before they cause a breakdown out on some lonely stretch of road. If you don't know the difference between a wrench and a pair of pliers, and couldn't care less, get to know your neighborhood bike mechanic.

Bike-Part Blues

When you buy a new bicycle, you're stuck with whatever parts it is sold with. You'd better be satisfied with the entire package; good bike parts are expensive and often not interchangeable among different brand frames. Although you can buy a frame and then add individual parts, the entire package will cost at least double that of a preassembled bike. Frames sold individually are usually hand-built and of good quality. If you're on a limited budget, stick with the package deal.

A 10-speed in the price range of $400 to $1000 will come with quality components that should last for years. You'll find these bikes equipped with brand-name components like Campagnolo, Sun Tour, Shimano, SR, Avocet, Zeus, TA, Sugino, Stronglight, Cinelli, Super Champion, Huret, TTT, Sakae, Mavic, Fiamme, Phil Wood, etc.

A word of caution about exotic components: A lot of super-light alloy parts, which appeal to the weight-conscious cyclist, are sold at bike shops. Some cyclists will do anything to remove a gram of weight, including drilling out their parts. Save your money. Extra-light parts often break under hard, prolonged use. And don't drill out your components to save a few grams. The weight savings doesn't amount to much more than that piece of toast you didn't eat for breakfast.

Wheels: A light set of wheels will do more to improve riding performance than any weight-savings elsewhere on the bike. Light wheels improve acceleration and handling. A set of custom-made, hand-built wheels will cost about $150. Ask your friendly bike mechanic to build you a pair.

Here is my set of "dream wheels."

Hub: Campagnolo Nuovo Record, low flange

Spokes: DT stainless steel, light gauge, double-butted

Spoke Pattern: 3 cross

Rim: Mavic Mod E-2 or Super Champion Gentleman, one-inch width

Tires: Specialized Turbo S clincher or 1 1/8-inch Specialized Touring II.

Some triathletes are serious enough about their cycling to order a special set of "time-trial" wheels with light rims and tires and fewer than 36 spokes. These wheels are structurally weaker than regular, 36-spoke wheels, so you must choose between the slight time savings you'll get from time-trial wheels and the increased risk of wheel failure. Time-trial wheels are fragile, spokes break and wheels don't stay true as long.

Tires: Veteran cyclists and racers recommend sewups, otherwise called tubulars, which have the inner tube sewn into the tire casing. After riding both sewups and the more conventional clincher tires, I have settled on clinchers — they're less hassle. I just don't have time to repair a punctured sewup. The entire process takes about 30 minutes and if the patch doesn't hold, which is often a problem, you have to repeat the entire maddening procedure of unsewing and sewing the casing. I used to throw away sewups that had flats, but the more expensive silk tires cost $36, so it gets expensive. I also don't recommend having two sets of wheels — one for racing (sewups) and one for training (clinchers). You become accustomed to the riding properties of your training tire, and switching to another tire for racing is risky business. For some experienced cyclists, though, this may not be a problem.

Many triathletes prefer to race on sewups, however, for their better performance and ease in changing. I don't think there is enough of a difference between clinchers and sewups to warrant the exclusive use of the latter. Here is a list of advantages and disadvantages of the two different kinds. You be the judge.

SEWUPS	CLINCHERS
1) expensive	1) affordable
2) time-consuming to patch	2) easy to patch
3) require messy glue	3) satisfactory handling and traction
4) less availability	4) readily available
5) easy to change	5) slightly heavier than sewups
6) lighter rims	6) slightly more rolling resistance
7) less rolling resistance	7) slightly heavier rims
8) lightweight	8) slightly harder to change a flat
9) superior handling and traction	

Flats: Flats have a special place in the hearts of cyclists. In accordance with Murphy's Law, they always occur at the worst possible time when it's least expected. Stories are legion of cyclists who train six months without a flat and then flat in a race.

To reduce the number of flats, follow some commonsense rules: 1) Keep your tires at their recommended pressure. Tires at low pressure have a greater chance of bottoming out, which means that the tube can be pinched against the rim when it hits a bump. The result is a "vampire" flat. 2) Be sure you have adequate rim tape. A spoke poking beyond the inside face of the rim can cause a flat. 3) Avoid riding through glass and potholes. The lighter the tire, the more chance it has of puncturing. The more you weigh, the heavier the tire you should ride. Tires that are 1 1/8-inch in diameter give more clearance between the rim and the road than 1-inch-diameter tires. More clearance means fewer chances of bottoming out.

Some riders take extra precautions, such as using tire savers. These loops of plastic-covered wire attach to the rear of the brake bolts; presumably, they skim the tire and pick up foreign objects before they can puncture the tube. I prefer to pray.

Water Bottles: Buy a bike with water-bottle braze-ons to avoid the inconvenience of clamps for water-bottle cages. Two bottle braze-ons enable you to mount two water-bottle cages. In a long race, two bottles are better than one.

Toe Clips and Toe Straps: Toe clips and toe straps will improve efficiency in pedaling. When strapped in, you can pull as well as push on the pedal. Also, the risk of a foot slipping off the pedal is reduced.

Brakes: Invest in a good set of side-pull brakes, such as Campagnolo, Modolo, Universal CX, Shimano Dura-Ace or Sun Tour Superbe. A brakeset like these costs between $60 and $120.

Seat: There's not a seat made that lets you feel comfortable after five hours of riding if you're not used to cycling, but the better brands for comfort and durability include Avocet, Brooks (leather), Concor and Turbo.

Cycling Shoes: Those cycling shoes that are fitted with cleats and have stiff soles will enhance comfort and cycling efficiency compared to tennis shoes. In a short bike ride during a triathlon, some competitors just wear their running shoes so they don't have to change during transition. But with running shoes, you will sacrifice efficiency and comfort, and add wear and tear on your running shoes.

Shorts: The trademark of riding shorts is a leather chamois sewn into the seat. The chamois increases comfort, absorbs sweat and reduces chafing. Riding shorts have no exposed seams that might cause chafing, and are usually made from wool, cotton, nylon or acrylic.

The cyclist's riding gear. 1) Silca floor pump 2) Water bottle 3) Kucharik leather helmet 4) Silca frame pump with Campagnolo steel pump head 5) Sidi cycling shoes 6) Tool bag 7) Sidi "booties" for cycling shoes 8) Cycling jersey and socks 9) Spare inner tube 10) Spare sew-up tire 11) Cycling gloves 12) Heart monitor 13) Cycling skin shorts 14) Protogs wool tights.

Cycling Gloves: If your hands usually become numb while cycling, wear padded cycling gloves, or else pad your handlebars. Numbness often results from applying too much weight to the handlebars, which pinches the ulnar nerve that runs through the base of your palms. Time on the bike will toughen your hand muscles, and gloves will help reduce numbness until then.

Helmet: In most triathlons, you are required to wear a helmet. Popular helmets include the plastic-shell Bell and Skid-Lid, and the Kucharik leather hairnet. In terms of protection from impact, many cyclists rate them in this order. But for comfort, the reverse order is true.

Skinsuit: The one-piece, nylon skinsuit was first used by speed skaters and bike racers, and now some triathletes are using it. Several brands are now made especially for triathletes. Originally designed to cut down on wind resistance and allow freedom of movement, the suit is valuable for triathletes in reducing time spent in transition. Wearing a suit throughout the event eliminates the need to change clothes.

Jersey: A jersey is probably the least necessary or useful item of clothing for a triathlete. T-shirts do just fine. I sometimes wear a cotton T-shirt on warm days, and Dave Scott wore a holey white T-shirt at the Ironman. For a long ride, however, rear pockets, which jerseys usually have, are handy for storing essentials like tools, a hat, food, gloves or a spare inner tube. Jerseys also fit snugly to reduce wind resistance and are tailored to cover your lower back when you bend over the bars.

Training Aids

Bad weather can prevent riding outside, but that doesn't mean you have to miss a workout on the bike. You can ride inside with the aid of a bike stand that you mount your bike on. The stand requires no more than removal of the front wheel to set up. Two popular stands are Racer-Mate and the Turbo-Trainer. Their sleek frames are light and portable. Each costs about $150.

Rollers are another alternative, but they have their drawbacks. For simulating riding conditions, they are superior to the stationary bike stands, but I don't think they give you as good of a workout. Rollers require skill at balancing, which, during a long workout, can become a chore. If your attention wanders for even a moment, you can go flying off. Rollers also don't give as much rolling resistance as do stationary stands.

Finally, to keep track of mileage and speed during the ride, a cyclo-computer, a miniature computer that attaches to the handlebars, is a useful purchase. The Cat-Eye and the Push, which are no bigger than the palm of your hand, calculate speed in mph, average speed over a course, maximum speed over a course, elapsed time and total mileage. They sell for about $60 each. More sophisticated and even smaller devices similar to these brands are being developed.

RUNNING

Before running became a general craze, you learned about running from your friendly high school coach. Armed with the inflexible philosophy that no pain means no gain, he ordered his thinclads onto the school's quarter-mile track for lengthy interval sessions. He learned about intervals from the Germans, who, with Nietzschean zeal, were known to flog themselves through an unending series of torturous interval sessions, like 20 x 440 followed by 10 x 880. Top that off with some lung-burners, 40 x 110. Little did the coach realize that his workouts were taken right from the training diary of Olympic gold medalist Emil Zatopek.

The coach always had sage words of advice about technique and form, which he administered loudly enough to impress the football coaches standing on the infield: "Lift those knees! Pump those arms!" But now, thanks to the running explosion, training is more sane, more humane. Feature-length articles, photo essays and running symposiums explaining the intricacies of training systems could fill an encyclopedia. As you consider technique, apply it to reducing your chances of injury. Overuse injuries from running, like shinsplints, sore knees, sciatica, Achilles tendinitis – the list goes on – are caused in part by improper gait.

Putting Your Best Foot Forward

During long runs, concentrate on form. Thinking about the motion of running is part of the evolutionary process to becoming a better runner.

Head. Keep it straight and steady. Look ahead and slightly down (to avoid potholes and landmines). Although Jim Ryun was the world-record holder in the mile, he wagged his head excessively (because of an inner ear problem). In the late 1960s, a lot of milers mistakenly wagged their heads as a result of studying Ryun's style

Torso. There are leaners and those who carry themselves ramrod straight. I prefer the slight forward lean, so I fall into the camp with Olympic Coach Brooks Johnson.

Arms. Keep your arms loose at your sides and bent at a 90-degree angle; arm motion should not cause your hands to cross your chest. During a long run, arms are rather unimportant appendages.

Stride. He who overstrides is lost. Overstriding is a major cause of leg injury. Your natural gait is your most efficient gait, and vice versa

Footstrike. Most novice runners have a heel-to-toe footstrike, but the evolutionary process will eventually have you running more on the balls of your feet. As you progress, there will be more spring in your gait, your calf muscles will strengthen and you will gain speed.

Over Hill and Dale. Unless your sport of origin is running, slow your pace when running downhill; the increased pounding you'll take is a sure way to get injured. Lower your arms at the elbows about 10 degrees and lean back if you want to slow down. Lean forward if you want to speed up. On the uphill, lift the knees and pump your arms. The steeper the hill, the more you lean into it. Shorten stride.

IF THE SHOE FITS, WEAR IT

A good pair of running shoes can mean the difference between injury and good health, although there are the rare exceptions. Abebe Bakila, two-time Olympic gold-medal winner, won the Rome Olympic marathon in his bare feet. And he did it running on cobblestone streets. Bakila was a poor Ethiopian farmer before he became a great runner, so he didn't know better, nor did he have the money to buy a pair of shoes. Unless you were raised without shoes, wear them.

Step one in buying the right shoe for you is to patronize your local running-shoe store. When I started running in 1969, selecting a running shoe was no problem. I had about five different models from which to choose, if I was willing to drive halfway across the state of Massachusetts to find a sporting goods shop that sold all five. Now I can drive to the nearest shopping

Former marathon world-record holder and triathlete Allison Roe displays excellent running form.

center and have the best running shoes in the world at my toe-tips. Their construction and materials are light-years better today than they were only five years ago.

Step two is to choose a training flat. Forget the racing flat, even for competition. The extra cushion in a training shoe will reduce the risk of injury. According to a shoe study by Peter Cavanagh at the Penn State Biomechanics Lab, if you were to switch from the best training flat to the worst racing flat, it would involve more than a 400 percent decrement in forefoot protection. Consider that with each footstrike, your body absorbs between two and three times its body weight.

On to the nitty gritty — choosing the right training flat. There is no easy answer, unless, of course, a shoe company supplies you with free shoes. If you're not that lucky, consider the following:

• Body Weight. Generally, the heavier you are, the more padding you need.

• Gait. Most runners strike heel first. Some runners, however land on the balls of their feet and hardly touch their heels. They need a shoe with good forefoot padding.

• Injury Background. If you're always sidelined with a nagging injury while wearing a particular shoe, dump it.

• Foot Structure. There are flat feet, medium-arch feet and high-arch feet. High-arch feet generally need a shoe with good flexibility, in preference to padding. Flat-footed runners need extra support.

• Old Shoes. Don't wear old running shoes; even if they don't look worn, they can be shot. The mid-sole material loses its resiliency after a while and thus has less shock absorbency. If your shoes show considerable wear in the heels after a short time, you probably have a severe biomechanical abnormality that requires correction. See a qualified sportsmedicine orthopedist or a podiatrist.

• Biomechanics. Orthopedists and podiatrists understand foot biomechanics. They can tell you if you have the dreaded overpronation, which is a cause for many injuries. You can identify overpronation by looking at the heels of your shoes. If they wear excessively on the inside within a short time, you are overpronating. Overpronation and other biomechanical problems can sometimes be corrected with shoe inserts called orthotics, which are usually made of molded plastic and fit unobtrusively inside the shoe. They aren't cheap, though; they can cost as much as $300 and come with no guarantees.

CLOTHING

• Socks. Some runners contend that running without socks reduces the chance of getting blisters. I agree. But if you want to wear socks, some are less prone to causing friction than others; it depends on their ability to absorb moisture. Wick socks — 60 percent orlon, 25 percent nylon and 5 percent other fabrics — are best for absorbing sweat, and thus reducing the instance of blisters.

● Shorts. Buy running shorts made of nylon; those with an inner lining are the most comfortable. Light, smooth nylon reduces chafing

● Singlet. Singlets used to be made entirely of nylon, until it was discovered that cotton mesh everywhere but over the chest was more comfortable. To avoid a lot of pain on a long run, no matter what kind of shirt you wear, it is often advisable to tape your nipples with Band-Aids.

● Hat. Hats shade the eyes and protect the head on a hot, sunny day. Dip your hat in cold water on a hot day to keep your head cool.

● Sweats. Baggy, gray sweats used to be all that was available. They cost about $15, and although they didn't look all that great, they kept you moderately warm. Now there are Gore-Tex nylon sweat suits that cost $160 and more. They let body moisture escape, keep out rain and retain body heat. If you can't afford Gore-Tex, dress in several layers of cotton to keep warm. Layers of light clothing are more effective at keeping you warm than a single heavy layer.

Expect to spend at least $45 on a pair of running shoes. Add another $45 to the rest of your clothing bill, if you skip the sweat suit.

4

Health vs. Fitness

My friend Zachary Minimus (a fictitious name) was an inexperienced, naive runner when he joined the cross-country team as a walk-on (no scholarship). Like all walk-ons, he hoped he could become good enough to make varsity. And like most American athletes, he had great expectations — fame, respect, success, Olympic glory and getting his face on a box of Wheaties. Like a lot of other athletes, too, Zack believed that the path to success was clear and straightforward: he would simply work his tail off. He believed in the promises of the banners plastered across the walls of the school's aging indoor track: "Success Through Sacrifice," "Heroes Are Made Not Born."

True to his vow, Zack did every workout the coach posted on the locker-room bulletin board. He would come back from 20-mile runs in the dead of winter, freezing and spent — too tired to fix dinner, too tired to shower. Although it was obvious to everyone on the team, including the coach, that Zack would never make varsity, nobody told him. So Zack wracked his body through one workout after another.

A little of Zachary Minimus is in all of us. In high school and college, everyone has dreams of being the best athlete. Many have said we live for our dreams. And it is probably just as well that in our youth we don't realize that success and ability are as much a factor of our parents' genes as they are of hard work. If we knew then what we know now, would we train as hard? Would we become cynics at a tender age?

There is a satisfying conclusion to the Zachary Minimus story. By reading about training principles at the school library, he found out what makes the body tick, and the factors that make some people Olympians and others sloggers. He discovered that what little natural speed he did have could not be markedly improved upon by training. As a result, he turned his attention from short cross-country races to the marathon. By the time he finished college, his PR was a respectable 2:40. Despite his biomechanical handicaps, Zack had reached his potential. And he never lost his love of running once he realized that rest was as important as hard work. He still runs today and still enjoys it thoroughly.

An athlete's genetic limitations include such factors as body type (ectomorph, endomorph, mesomorph), muscle-fiber ratio (fast-twitch vs. slow-twitch), maximum oxygen uptake and genetics itself. Each of us is born with certain physical characteristics. If we are lucky, they will be the right combination for greatness. But whatever our natural ability, only through proper training can we achieve our potential. It is also through training that we are made aware of our limitations, at which time we can adapt or alter our goals. If you can't run under six minutes for the mile after a year of training, there is no reason to believe that more practice will make you a top miler. Your genetic potential will probably be reached in a longer race where endurance is a factor.

Although your natural ability becomes a known element as you age, the ingredients for maximizing performance, even with a sound training program, still include intangibles — injury-free training, mental fortitude and luck. Marathoner Frank Shorter would not have been given the incentive to be an Olympian had he relied strictly on scientific data. His maximum oxygen uptake, or VO_2 max, at 71.3, was low by world-class standards. Most Olympians have a VO_2 max of between 80 and 85. But Shorter trained so efficiently that he was able to sustain a higher level of oxygen consumption for an extended period.

Traditionally, drive and determination have been associated with the success of athletes. This pursuit of excellence is good as long as it is not overzealous or mindless. Overachievers often leave their best efforts on the training grounds and not at the races. The risks of overtraining are well known, the results all too familiar. Derek Clayton, former world-record holder in the marathon, paid the price of megamileage workouts with a dozen operations on his legs. Dave Bedford set a 10,000-meter world record on megamileage and then retired at a young age, burned out and injured. When Bill Rodgers was running as many as 138 miles a week in 1977, ambitious runners wore out their shoes and their bodies trying to match him. Cyclists did the same to overtake France's Bernard Hinault, and swimmers piled up yardage to erase Mark Spitz' records.

Those who try to emulate the elite athlete are asking for trouble. They are committing a cardinal sin in training — listening to another athlete's body instead of their own. Recovery time from workouts is not a common denominator. Some athletes need only 18 to 24 hours between hard workouts; most need between 48 and 72 hours. The amount of time a body needs to recuperate from a workout is not to be construed as a sign of weakness, but as a fact of life.

Understand the basis of the Adaptation Syndrome in training and you will succeed at the triathlon. In three words it means: stress, then rest. Once you adapt to one level of stress, you are ready to go to a higher level of stress. But you must first adapt before continuing up the ladder of fitness. If you skip steps and try taking them two at a time, you are more likely to trip and fall back down the ladder. For years, athletes have realized the importance of intense training to yield dramatic gains, but they have always shunned or ignored the need for rest.

You may have been trained by your school coach that the old saying, "no pain, no gain," is true because it makes you stronger mentally. The coach's ultra-hard workouts were more for building character than for physiological adaptation to stress. But like most of the coaches out of the 1950s, he did not know about the Adaptation Syndrome's call for rest. A lot of young athletes trained by these coaches suffered injuries brought on by lack of rest or from "burnout."

Today we're seeing these same people starting an exercise program and falling into the Overtraining Syndrome. The once-young athletes, in their thirties and forties now, still adhere to their coach's "no pain, no gain" philosophy. They are the ones who, after only a few weeks of exercise, give up in frustration. They expect dramatic improvement overnight. Remember, though, that the fitness ladder must be taken one step at a time, whether you're a neophyte athlete or an Olympian.

I learned too late in my running career that less is more, that those extra miles I tried to squeeze in each week dragged me down. Hard workouts are necessary, but not in concentrated doses without rest. It was easy to do at the time, however, because the more I trained, the more important training became. And like most athletes, I love to work out.

My theory about why so many athletes overtrain is linked to research breakthroughs in the last decade concerning chemicals produced in the brain. I think that athletes are in a way "drugged" by their training, and that the more they work out, the more they need the body's naturally occurring "drugs" — endorphins, otherwise known as the "morphine within." Beta-endorphin is thought to be between five and 10 times more potent than morphine.

Dr. Avram Goldstein, professor of pharmacology at Stanford University, says in the March 1978 issue of *The Sciences,* "The most clearly understood action of enkephalin [a type of endorphin] is in the spinal cord, where small enkephalin-containing neurons impinge on the terminals of the nerve cells that convey pain information to the spinal cord." Dr. Goldstein, director of the Addiction Research Foundation in Palo Alto, California, is doing research on endorphins and their effects on the mind.

Some scientists believe that endorphins are responsible for what's popularly known as the "runner's high." Many runners describe feelings of euphoria and heightened awareness during and after long runs; some have gone so far as to call it a "religious experience."

But this doesn't answer my theory of addiction to training. According to Dr. Goldstein, "Unfortunately, the endorphins not only have the pharmacologic actions of morphine, they also produce tolerance and physical dependence in a typical opiate manner." My interpretation, not necessarily Dr. Goldstein's, is that the more we train, the more endorphins we pump into our systems, and the greater our tolerance to training becomes. We're so doped up that we may think we feel better than ever during heavy training when actually we're on the verge of illness or injury. Endorphins may work for the mind, but they don't protect the body. Dr. Goldstein puts it another way in *The Healing Arts:* "Maybe we all carry around our own dope in our heads."

Because you are training for a triathlon, and are probably already an athlete hooked on training, I suspect you'll never need to worry about undertraining.

HEALTH VS. FITNESS CHART

Fitness brings many physiological benefits: a larger, stronger heart that can pump more blood with each stroke, greater oxygen uptake, improved blood circulation, resistance to illness and disease and a leaner, more efficient body. Diet, rest and mental attitude will also affect your life in relation to your training. But the athlete in pursuit of peak performance reaches a point of diminishing returns when the Adaptation Syndrome training stairway dead-ends. At that point, your body says, "Stop! I can't handle any more stress. This is my biological limit. You're going to have to live with it." It's not that easy, though, because the mind is stubborn. It replies in outrage, "What da ya mean, the limit! I can handle much more than you are willing to take. You're weak. I'll show you." The athlete proceeds to push himself beyond the threshold and into the dark, menacing world of illness and injury.

I have devised a Health vs. Fitness chart (see Fig. 1) to depict the relationship between health and fitness. It might help you

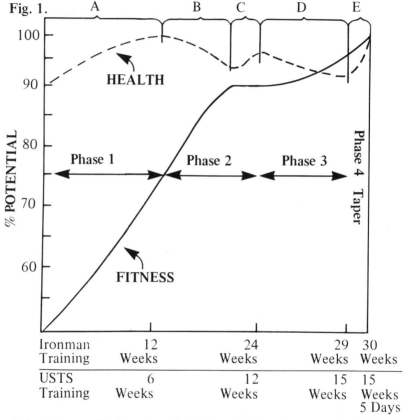

Fig. 1.

Ironman Training	12 Weeks	24 Weeks	29 Weeks	30 Weeks
USTS Training	6 Weeks	12 Weeks	15 Weeks	15 Weeks 5 Days

A: As your aerobic base is established and fitness improves, health also improves.

B: As the intensity of workouts increases during the Buildup phase (Phase 2) and fitness improves even more, health drops slightly, increasing susceptibility to flu, colds, irritability, insomnia.

C: Therefore, during the last few weeks of Phase 2, back off to 60 or 70 percent to allow health to catch up again and prepare for the Peak phase.

D: Once again, during Phase 3, the body is under stress to recover from workouts — health is sacrificed.

E: Hence, the importance of the Taper, Phase 4. It allows a short period of rest so that all systems are fully recovered and ready for the race.

There will be further discussion of the training phases in Chapter 6. See Fig. 4, pg. 91.

avoid falling down the fitness ladder. Note that in time frame A, health and fitness improve simultaneously. Your ability to ward off infection, metabolize impurities and waste products and resist illness is enhanced with improved fitness. But at some point, shown in time frame B, your fitness plateaus. If you continue training at the same intensity, your health will deteriorate (see Fig. 2). That's why, during time frame C, I recommend that

Fig. 2.

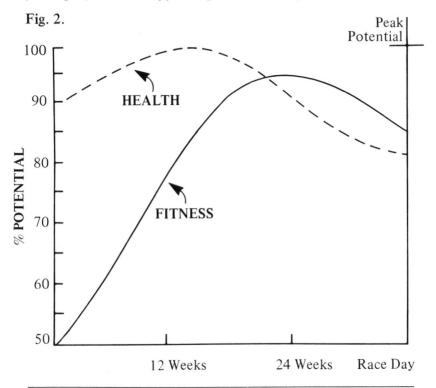

This graph shows the results of overtraining. During the first few weeks or months of training, fitness and health improve together. Later, as workouts become more demanding, health will begin to falter if adequate recovery is not allowed. Eventually, illness or injury will disrupt training, and your fitness will also begin to decline. If you train through this, you'll only make things worse. Even if you make it to the starting line, your performance will be less than it could be.

you back off from your training for two to three weeks to allow your health to recover for the final peak training. This is the time to give those aches and pains a chance to dissipate by resting more and working out less. Once at this level, you can maintain your condition with only 40 percent of the effort.

During time frame D you are training at your highest intensity to capture that final 10 percent needed for peak fitness. Your health declines again, but the taper, time frame E, should bring your health back to 100 percent.

The race will have immediate deleterious effects on your health and fitness, so you should give yourself a well-deserved rest following an Ironman-type triathlon. If training is resumed too soon after the race, both health and fitness will decline. The mistake many triathletes make after finishing one triathlon is to grab for more right away with the intention of riding through the next event on the crest of their good condition.

Ernst van Aaken, a well-known German running coach, suggests that racing and speed training should not constitute more than 2 to 5 percent of your training time. Using this formula, a triathlete is limited to one racing hour in as few as 20 (2 percent) and as much as 50 training hours (5 percent). Don't race again until you have trained this number of hours. Assuming you need three hours to complete a USTS race, you should not race before accumulating 60 hours of training. If you train an average of 15 hours a week, you would not compete again for four weeks.

Tailor this health-and-fitness curve to your body's needs, and remember that the process of increasing fitness occurs on a weekly or monthly basis. Don't expect overnight improvement, even if you are an elite triathlete. Gains are often made in a "ratchet mode" — two steps forward and one step back.

Although I am not opposed to using mileage as a measuring stick for fitness, realize that it can give false readings. There is no accounting for the quality of those miles or the toll they exact. What if that 10-mile run was at an elevation of 7000 feet on a steep mountain trail? What if your long swim was in the ocean where you had to battle waves and cold temperatures? You can guard against misinterpretation of mileage totals by writing in your training diary how hard you thought the workout was — hard, medium-hard or easy. Your foremost goal in a week should be to put in a certain number of hard workouts, and cumulative mileage should be secondary to that. You know best what constitutes a hard workout — not your best friend, not your coach, not even your mother. I am not purposely avoiding the issue of how to train by omitting a day-by-day workout schedule (see Appendix for a sample training diary); rather, I am saving your hide by not listing one. Make up your workouts to suit your own needs. Don't enslave yourself to someone else's workout program.

Maintaining a log, or better yet, a journal (with mileage, times, weather conditions and how you felt) will help you learn from experience and better plan for future gains. Many top triathletes do not have a written program they adhere to; instead, they continuously shuffle workouts around their weaknesses, the need to back off for a few days or the weather. However, they usually have in mind total weekly or biweekly mileage and intensity goals based on the patterns of previous weeks or months and their capacity for recovering and benefiting from workouts.

STRENGTH, ENDURANCE, MENTAL FORTITUDE AND SPEED

When planning triathlon workouts, keep in mind these four training concepts: muscle strength, muscle endurance, mental fortitude and speed. The nature and intensity of your workouts will determine which area is stressed.

Strength

By strength, I don't mean that you should join a health club and start pumping iron. Bulking up is not a requisite for success in the triathlon. I'm talking about toning the muscles so that they will be at their greatest efficiency in their "power band."

Before you assume that power band refers to the latest punk rock group, let me clarify. The power band is the range in which your muscles are most efficient during a given motion. In cycling, for example, the ideal power band is to have maximum output throughout the turn of the crank. It is not just during the downstroke that you exert force, but during the upstroke, too, when you pull up on the pedal. Many cyclists automatically limit their power band by not using toe clips, toe straps and cleated cycling shoes. Without them, you can't pull up on the pedal.

Strength gains are most easily achieved if you work out using the hard/easy system: train hard one day or several days and then back off and rest. As I mentioned, how long you rest will vary according to inborn characteristics. Putting in hard or even medium-hard workouts day in and day out for a week and then resting on Sunday, for example, invites injury. The body needs more time to rest than one day a week.

Repetition is vital to improving your power band and strength. Neuromuscular patterning develops with repetition of a movement such as, say, spinning while pedaling. Neural activity tends to follow pathways that have already been traveled, and these pathways become stronger as the movement is repeated. If you habitually fail to follow through on your stroke in the swim, your mind will eventually think of it as normal and correct. Once the problem is pointed out by a coach, it will take a concerted effort to unlearn your habit and develop a more efficient stroke. Swimming, in particular, relies on neuromuscular patterning. Someone who has swum for years will tell you that his movements come "naturally," but to the novice, each stroke must be consciously guided by the brain through all phases. Keeping track of all four limbs can be taxing. And as you age, the muscles become less limber and coordination declines.

Your most efficient power band on the bicycle can be found by choosing the proper gears, which allow you to maintain that power band on uneven terrain. Neophyte cyclists, however, sometimes don't know what the right cadence is. I think it's the pace you feel most comfortable at. If you start breathing heavily, it's obvious that you're spinning too fast. If your legs begin to tie up, you're pushing a gear that's too big.

Strength in running can be gained by doing track intervals. The distance of each interval should be at least 880 yards and can be as much as one mile. Long-distance intervals do more for recruiting slow-twitch muscle fibers than wind-sprints. Hill running and short road races will also help improve your strength.

Endurance

Muscle endurance is achieved by going on long workouts, those that deplete all of your stored glycogen and leave you with mostly fat to burn. Count on two hours or more to reach this stage. At that point, you will make your greatest gains toward building muscle endurance. These workouts not only simulate race conditions, but also bring about physiological changes in your body.

The wall (running), bonk (cycling), and bear (swimming), all refer to the same thing: the critical period when the body shifts from burning glycogen to burning fat. There is much emphasis today on delaying the point at which the body is depleted of glycogen, which is accomplished by saturating the muscles with glycogen, a process known as carbohydrate-loading. The concept is sound, but it has a built-in limitation. No matter how much you eat, the body cannot store enough glycogen to train long hours without burning fat. Once you've reached your dietary goal, the path to improved endurance is through proper training. The best workouts, the ones that I call fat-burning workouts, are those that force the body to switch from glycogen to fat for fuel. The body contains protein-like substances called enzymes that speed the chemical process of converting fat to energy. When the body has to burn fat, it recruits this army of special enzymes, and the more often they are recruited (within the boundaries of maintaining health), the faster they will be able to break down fat.

Neuromuscular patterning is as important in endurance as in strength. There will be times during the triathlon when you feel so tired and are in such pain that your actions are more like those of an automoton; your body is on automatic pilot. The more often you simulate that uncomfortable situation during training, the better prepared you will be in competition, when you are not only trying to survive but pushing yourself to your outer limits.

In the late stage of a long triathlon, your muscles respond by summoning other fibers to do some of the work for the fatigued endurance muscles. Because slow-twitch fibers are the busiest during an endurance event, rather than the fast-twitch fibers, they are the ones generally "trained." Fast-twitch fibers, which are in every muscle, are recruited to pick up the slack. Conversely, slow-twitch fibers cannot be recruited to perform the functions of fast-twitch fibers.

Mental Fortitude

Mental fortitude, less quantifiable or qualifiable than muscle strength or endurance, is considered by many to be equal to, if not more important than, physical endurance. In the Olympic Games, some argue, the superior athlete of the day is the one who is the toughest mentally.

You can't condition yourself mentally by following a prescribed training program. You don't buy tape-recorded messages or wear fancy equipment to improve your mental abilities. The only way I know to become stronger mentally is to pay the price from time to time in the workout.

Back in the 1950s, a group of runners experimented with what they called a "breakthrough workout," which they did on their way to peaking for an important event. In that workout, usually a session of endless intervals, they pushed themselves to the brink of exhaustion. Subsequent workouts seemed easy, they reported, even those they had once considered hard. And in the heat of competition, they never lacked for mental willpower. Performances improved.

Focus and concentration are other intangibles of mental fortitude. In their martial arts, the Japanese and Chinese place a high priority on concentration. The karate expert, excluding all external stimuli, focuses his thoughts on a brick to break it with his hand. Bruce Lee could knock a man down with his one-inch punch. The triathlete also must concentrate during competition, but the sport demands a slightly less intense concentration spread out over a much longer period of time. Right after the Ironman triathlon, friends came up to me to say that they had yelled encouragement to me during the last miles of the run. I had been so intent on concentrating, however, that I had no memory of them.

Speed

The word speed, when mentioned in relation to an athletic event, immediately conjures up images of a sprinter flying down a 100-meter straightaway. The same goes for endurance triathletes, too; we often describe the leaders as being very fast. The two concepts of speed, however, are entirely different. The sprinter's effort is anaerobic — without air. In a triathlon, even the best triathletes hardly, if ever, reach anaerobic effort. The triathlon should be 100 percent aerobic — in the presence of oxygen. The best pace in the triathlon is that at which you are as close as possible to your anaerobic threshold, but never beyond it. The steady, aerobic pace is the most efficient. Short bursts of speed might improve your position temporarily, but they will tire you quickly, throw off your pace and disrupt concentration.

Anaerobic workouts, however, do have a place in training for a triathlon. Short periods of anaerobic work, such as during an interval session or fartlek, will improve overall conditioning and accustom you to the feeling of going anaerobic. As your condition improves, your anaerobic threshold will rise.

A sprinter probably would not make a great triathlete for the precise reason that he is a good sprinter. Sprinters are born with a higher proportion of fast-twitch muscle fibers than slow-twitch. Fast-twitch fibers work more efficiently in the absence of oxygen, while slow-twitch fibers are most efficient in the presence of oxygen. But while the sprinter could train to be a good triathlete, the good triathlete would have a much harder time becoming a good sprinter. Fast-twitch muscle fiber can be trained more readily to function in the presence of oxygen than slow-twitch can adjust to functioning without oxygen. Many great middle-distance runners, who usually have an even proportion of fast-twitch to slow-twitch muscle fibers, often branch out to become national-class marathoners.

If you lack speed and have never trained beyond the point of establishing an aerobic base, you can improve. Simply train with speed in mind and concentrate on short, fast workouts.

The young triathlete should work on speed because he can gain the most from speed training at an early age.

ALTITUDE TRAINING

When the J. David team, a group of elite triathletes sponsored by the J. David money management firm in Southern California, took a week-long bike excursion in the Sierra Nevada in 1982, they weren't out to see the scenery. The team wanted to train at high altitude in preparation for the October Ironman. They believed that training at altitude would lead to better performances.

Although physiologists still haven't pinpointed the benefits of training at altitude, athletes who do so claim that it's responsible for their lower times at sea level. Physiologists believe that the increased production of hemoglobin from altitude training (beginning at about 4000 feet) accounts for the better times. Hemoglobin carries oxygen to the muscles via the blood. The increased demands on the body for air at high altitude cause additional stress and increase the amount of hemoglobin in the blood. In a low-altitude competition, the high-altitude-trained body can thus supply more oxygen to the muscles. Most authorities agree that several weeks of training at altitude are required to gain these benefits.

The main benefit from training at altitude is its eventual effect of reducing wear and tear on muscles and connective tissues. Because it takes less work to obtain the same benefits in high altitude training than in low altitude, you don't need to work out as often or for as long.

BLOOD POOLING

With exercise, blood circulates to the muscles in use more efficiently, supplying more oxygen and removing lactic acid and other waste products that result from muscle use. The increased flow of blood to a region of the body is called blood pooling.

Blood pooling is critical for the triathlete because he is practicing sports that involve different body parts. Swimming, for example, concentrates blood in the working arm, chest and shoulder muscles. In the next event, a run or ride, the blood is required in the legs, not the upper body. Many triathletes complain that once they begin cycling after a swim, their legs feel dead for several minutes before they regain some liveliness. The legs are used sparingly during the swim, and as a result, blood flows from the legs to the arms. Once out of the water and on the bike, it takes several minutes or more to get sufficient blood to the legs. Swim/bike combination workouts will help the body become more efficient at transferring blood from the upper body to the legs.

Blood pooling is less of a factor during the bike/run transition, but it is still important. The blood must move from the leg muscles used in cycling to the leg muscles used in running.

HEART RATE AND TRAINING

Monitoring the heart is the athlete's most accurate way to determine fitness and degree of effort and recovery in a workout. A pounding heart is a sure sign that you're putting forth your best effort. As athletic performance and fitness improve, the body can perform for a longer period of time and at a higher heart rate. In addition the resting heart will beat more slowly and forcefully to maintain blood circulation. Of prime importance in training is strengthening the heart so that it can pump more blood to the oxygen-starved muscles, and do so with fewer contractions.

If you know your heart rate during a workout and keep track of it for the duration of your training program, you can trace the overall improvement in your fitness level. You can also use your heart rate during interval workouts to find out how much time you should rest between repetitions. And on a daily basis, your resting pulse is an indication of whether you have recovered sufficiently from a workout to do another. If your pulse is seven to 10 beats higher than normal (your pulse rate before getting out of bed in the morning), you know you should either go for an easy workout or take the day off.

To determine your resting pulse, place two fingers over the artery in your wrist or on the carotid artery in the neck under the chin. Count the beats for 30 seconds and double the result to find your heart rate. During exercise, count your pulse for only 10 seconds, and then multiply the result by six to find your exercising heart rate. Your heart rate declines rapidly when you stop exercising to take your pulse.

Humans have a theoretical maximum heart rate of about 200 beats per minute. No matter how hard you train or how healthy you are, this rate declines with age. Use this formula to find your theoretical maximum heart rate: 220 - AGE = MAXIMUM HEART RATE. If you are less than 20, your maximum rate is still 200.

You can use your maximum heart rate to find your recommended training rate, or your target training rate. The beginning exerciser should work out at 65 percent of his maximum heart rate. For example, a 30-year-old's target training rate is 123:

220 - 30 = 190 x .65(%) = 123. As you become more fit, your heart gets stronger and can sustain a higher rate. A world-class athlete can train at 85 percent of his maximum heart rate for many hours.

Another method to determine your target training heart rate uses your resting pulse (RP), yet another factor in evaluating fitness. Following are the formulas for beginning, trained and world-class athletes:

BEGINNER

(Max HR - RP) x .65 + RP = Training Rate

TRAINED ATHLETE

(Max HR - RP) x .75 + RP = Training Rate

TOP TRIATHLETE

(Max HR - RP) x .85 + RP = Training Rate

TARGET TRAINING RATE

Maintain your target training rate during time trials, LSD or combination workouts for longer periods of time. During interval workouts, you should exercise well above your target training rate for short time spans.

Heart rate can be used to determine your recovery time between repetitions during intervals. After each hard effort, the heart rate follows a typical pattern of falling quickly and then leveling off for several minutes before gradually returning to its resting rate. Many athletes mark the plateau (whatever that heart rate is) as a sign that short-term recovery is complete and they are ready for the next interval. To find your plateau, take your heart rate for six seconds at a time every 15 or 30 seconds. The result should look something like the graph in Figure 3.

In this example, Zack Minimus did a work interval at 170 beats per minute and found his resting plateau to be 110 beats per minute. For this workout, he rests one minute between intervals. The time factor in the plateau varies according to your condition and the nature and intensity of the interval.

Fig. 3.

HEART RATE FOLLOWING HARD EFFORT

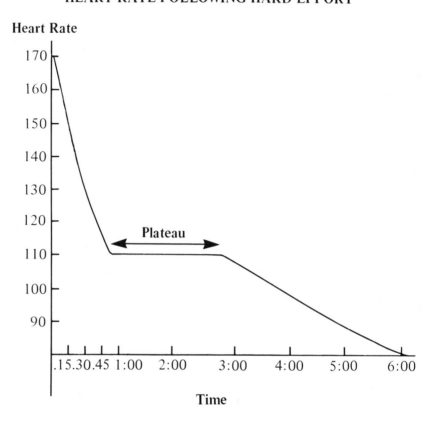

5

Training Strategy

Triathlon training is sometimes so uncertain that it bears similarity to the mirror maze at an amusement park: The great number of reflections is so bewildering that finding the way out is a matter of groping along and bumping into glass until you find the exit. Triathlon-training advice is often a maze of misinformation, too — contradictory and untested. We have yet to find the Arthur Lydiard of the triathlon, so we continue to search for the right formula. The most erudite apothecary would have a hard time brewing up a more fiendish formula. Triathlon workouts are complicated by the need to train for three — not one — sports, and you have to strive for excellence in each. The triathlon, at least in theory, is balanced equally so that one sport doesn't dominate another.

A new terminology has evolved to describe triathlon training: combination workouts — a single workout that combines two or more sports; cross-training — training in two or more sports with the intention of improving in one or more sports; and sport of origin — the triathlete's sport before coming to the triathlon.

Most important, training strategy is changing to suit the needs of the triathlete. In the past, triathletes have trained like runners, like cyclists and like swimmers. Now they are training like triathletes. Although there are obvious similarities in training methods, the triathlete must divorce himself from some of the basic training precepts of the single sports.

Before launching a training program, the triathlete should consider his goals and lifestyle. Does he want to be competitive? If so, he will need to spend more time training. Does he want to take on the Ironman or a similar event? That will take the supreme sacrifice in time and money. What about other interests, like family, job and friends? When do you train if you work all day? If you can only work out in the morning, is this the time of your physical peak? Can you afford the time to train and the cost of a pool fee, running shoes and bike parts?

Narrowing the Choices

Once you have decided on the goal and the amount of time you can allow for training, the next step is to train as efficiently as possible. This calls for you to 1) be impressive but comfortable in your strongest event (sport of origin); 2) be consistent in your next strongest event; and 3) be smartest in your weakest event.

Other factors will help you narrow down your training strategy, some of which follow:

● Concentrate on your weakest event. For most triathletes, that will be swimming and cycling.

● Restrict workouts to once or, at the most, twice a day. A few hard workouts in a week is more valuable than a week of solid workouts of medium difficulty. Remember, hard/easy.

● Combination workouts should follow a logical order, which is dictated by the sequence of events in the race you are training for. If the sequence is swim, bike, run, there is no sense in cycling and then swimming in a single workout; rather, you should swim and then ride.

● Restrict workouts combining all three sports to time trials on selected occasions.

● Plan to do half of your training in a single workout in a single sport.

● Combination workouts are valuable in reducing breakdowns from too much running and helping the body adapt to blood pooling. For example, if you swim and then run, you don't have to run as far to get an equivalent workout of only running. The combination workouts save the legs from wear and tear and possible injury.

● Make the most of your setting and climate. If you live near the hills, train in the hills. If you live in a cold climate, buy a stationary bike stand like the one described in Chapter 3.

● You have not trained adequately in a sport if you do not feel comfortable in it.

● Your hardest workouts should incorporate some cycling or swimming to reduce the risk of overuse injury from running.

SPORT BY SPORT

Swimming

Because of the nature of swimming and the need for efficient technique, quality workouts are more important than quantity workouts. If your sport of origin is swimming, however, you can continue to do your long, hard workouts in the pool until you are comfortable with the other sports.

Strength is of little use in swimming if style is inefficient. The runner or cyclist must train wisely in the swim, not blindly. Learn from a competent instructor. Covering the distance is not as important as doing it as quickly and efficiently as possible.

Cycling

The bike ride is usually the longest event, so your initial training rides should emphasize length and steady pace before speed. Because of the length of the ride, a minor inefficiency, such as pushing the wrong gear, can be magnified out of proportion. During workouts, concentrate on pedaling at all times, especially on hard, long workouts or time trials.

The triathlete rider is a time-trial specialist, not a bike racer. Concerned with steady pace, time-trial riders generally push bigger gears than racers. Other reasons for pushing big gears: 1) Spinning, although it can be easier on the joints and connective tissues, is not economical for slow-twitch muscle fibers, which endurance athletes have more of than fast-twitch fibers. 2) The triathlon is not a bike race requiring quick acceleration to catch breakaways (using low gears). 3) Pushing at a slightly lower rpm/slightly bigger gear more closely recreates the calf and thigh muscle tension experienced in running. Remember – most triathlons are swim, bike, run. I suggest maintaining a cadence of between 70 and 90 rpm.

Learn to ride long and ride consistently. Ride with an eye on the clock; kicking back and coasting can waste a lot of time. Always ride at or near race pace on flat courses, and learn to love hills.

Running

You don't need a Ph.D. in physical education to know that by the end of the triathlon, during the run, you're going to be tired. Jackson Browne's song aptly describes the feeling – "Running on Empty."

Neophyte runners must develop a base. There is usually a breaking-in period that all runners go through, a time during which the body adapts to the stresses of running. Injuries, usually minor, are not uncommon. After this base stage, injuries will be less frequent and you will not need to spend as much time training.

No matter how slow the pace, keep running. Walking, even though you may have a longer stride, is slower.

In the Ironman-type triathlon, pace — not speed — is important. Olympic cyclist John Howard trained for and won his second Ironman by running at an 8:00-mile pace, rarely faster. He knew that by the time the marathon came around, he would be too tired to go any faster. He thus learned pace and neuromuscular patterning and reduced his chances of injury by avoiding speedwork. Remember, the main source of energy at the running stage is fats.

6

Workouts and a Plan for Peak Performance

In this chapter, I'll describe several different types of workouts and their advantages. Whether you're Zachary Minimus or Kathleen McCartney, these workouts are applicable. I also provide a four-phase plan for peak performance in an Ironman or USTS triathlon. For shorter triathlon distances, the strategy is basically the same, but alter the time frame to suit your needs.

A nice feature of triathlon training is that it enables you to enjoy three popular sports. When you become mentally or physically tired from one, you can turn to another. And that's just one more reason why you might find yourself training too much. It's so easy to get wrapped up in the thrill of improving that the last thing you want to do is rest.

Recently I read a portion of the training diary of top American miler Steve Scott. I was not surprised to see that he rested on days when he felt tired, even if he had planned a workout. Scott is a smart athlete who has rarely been injured and can peak at the right time. Rather than going out for a scheduled interval session, he would just stay in bed when he felt tired.

Take a lesson from Scott. When adverse training conditions are unavoidable, weigh the pros and cons before launching into the workout. If you have a sore throat, should you go through with your planned swim or take the day off? If it's raining, should you cancel the bike ride and go for a short run instead? If you have a sore knee, should you scrap the run and go for a swim?

I am the first to admit that during my running years, I ran no matter how bad I felt, no matter how deep the snowdrifts, and I usually regretted it afterward. When people ask me if I would have trained differently if I knew then what I know now, I answer emphatically, "yes!" In training, quality supersedes quantity. I fell into the trap of overtraining when I was preparing for the first Ironman and came down with four colds. But I played it smart for the second Ironman and never got sick. The reason? I hadn't overtrained. The lessons learned: 1) When you go hard, you go hard. 2) When you rest, you rest hard. Don't be afraid to take a day off when you feel stale. 3) Maintain technique and form throughout the workout. 4) Three good workouts in a week yield more than six or seven mediocre ones. 5) Treat all minor injuries as potential major injuries.

THE WORKOUTS

Workouts are divided into three categories based on what phase of training you're in. Carefully compare the categories with the four-phase plan to peak performance. You'll see that the category of workout is dependent upon the phase you're in.

Category 1: Long, steady distance (LSD)

Long, steady distance is work done at less than 75 percent of your maximum heart rate. Workouts emphasize aerobic development to establish a base. Benefits:

1) Builds endurance base in early training stage.
2) Introduces triathlete to physical and mental stress of long distances.
3) Helps establish and maintain form over long distances.
4) Trains body to burn fat in later stages of race.
5) Familiarizes athlete with different sports and their biomechanical differences.

Swim: A swim of at least 1000 yards. I would occasionally swim as much as 5000 meters in a single workout. You can break up a one-mile swim into 9 x 200 yards, stopping five to 10 seconds to check your pulse, look at the clock, or just break the monotony. A two-mile swim could be done as 7 x 500 yards with a 10- to 20-second rest. Breaking up the workout gives you a better feel for pace and helps you keep track of strokes more easily.

Bike: Beginners should ride at least one hour; experienced riders, three to five hours. The long ride should eventually equal that of your race distance. Fatigue factors familiar to cyclists — sore butt, sore legs, sore back — don't usually set in until at least an hour into the ride. If you're training for the Ironman, the more 100-mile rides you put in, the better. Of course, give yourself adequate rest between rides.

Run: Non-runners should start modestly, taking long runs of about six miles. Weekly mileage increases should not be more than 10 percent of the previous week's total. To prepare for an Ironman-type triathlon, I recommend a 20-mile run if you have never run that far before. This is the distance at which most runners hit the wall.

Swim/Ride: The swim/ride workout prepares you for the effects of blood pooling, and should be done occasionally. I find it necessary to do a minimum of 1000 yards in the pool to get full benefit once on the bike. The critical training period is the first half-hour of cycling. Possibilities: 1000-yard swim/ 20-mile ride; 3000-yard swim/ 50-mile ride, and so on.

Swim/Run: This workout has the same benefit as the swim/ ride combination. It allows you to benefit from running fewer miles because you are already tired.

Ride/Run: With the bike/run workout, leg muscles will adjust to the switch from riding to running. The long ride/short run is a favorite of mine. No matter how short the run, I always made a point of running after a ride.

Category 2: Intervals (SPEED)

Category 2 workouts are done at faster or harder pace than race pace. All or part of these workouts should be performed at the anaerobic threshold, generally at a rate above 80 percent of your maximum heart rate. Major emphasis is on strength. Benefits:

1) Works you harder than a race does.

2) Reaching maximum heart rate trains the body to handle brief periods of "worst case" situations.

3) Recruits fast-twitch fibers during long, hard workouts.

Swim: Do 50-meter or 100-meter repeats. Use the clock to indicate when to go, say every 60 or 120 seconds. Go hard in the intervals because the heart recovers quickly in the water. Do at least 10, and as many as 50.

Hypoxic swims are done at less than optimum breathing intervals. This training method elevates the heart rate without taxing the muscles as much as they would be normally. The effect is similar to altitude training. The workout also encourages the triathlete to become comfortable with breathing from either side, thus reducing the chances of panicking when an occasional breath is missed in a race.

In the hypoxic swim workout, try to breathe only every three to five strokes. Sets of 50- and 100-yard intervals are sufficient to elevate the heart rate. This is a good time to practice bilateral breathing — breathing from one side and then breathing from the opposite side in constant rotation. Bilateral breathing is useful in competition when you want to view competitors on both sides of you, when wave action hinders viewing from one side or when you are trying to find your way on the course.

Pull sets are intervals done with each or all of the following: pull buoy, hand paddles and inflated tube. This is a valuable workout for the triathlete because the arms are his major source of strength. The kick is not developed during these workouts.

Kick sets, which should be done only occasionally, teach the triathlete to keep the lower half of his body horizontal in the water. Propulsion is not the main goal because the legs should be saved for the ride and run. A kickboard is useful when practicing kick sets.

In swimming, the term "intervals" usually refers to the rest intervals rather than the work intervals. When doing short intervals, be sure to elevate the heart rate high enough to exceed race pace and allow enough time between efforts to reach the resting plateau for your heart rate. Some swimmers use a constant rest principle; they swim 100 meters and rest 15 seconds. Others use a constant starting point; they swim 100 meters every time the clock hits two minutes. With this method, which works best for me, the faster you swim, the longer your rest period, and it puts pressure on to keep the workout going.

Swim/Ride: The swim/ride in Category 2 is the same as that in Category 1, but it requires harder effort. Since water takes heat from the legs, to reduce the risk of injury after the swim, you should spin (maintain a high rpm — 95 to 120) the first mile or so of the ride to get warmed up. Practice making a quick change into your cycle clothing.

Ride: The best way I know to do a fartlek ride — an unstructured interval workout — is to ride with fellow triathletes or cyclists. Invariably, there will be competition, like a sprint to the top of the hill or to the city limits sign. Such speed play is a valuable way to stress the heart in a relaxed, unstructured atmosphere, which is uncommon in timed intervals. The disadvantage is that you never know how hard you have worked out.

Hill climbs are good for getting in a short, hard workout. Find a hill 100 to 200 meters in length and try to climb it in

This bike is mounted on a Turbo Trainer. A favorite workout of mine includes the use of a heart monitor and portable tape cassette.

the biggest gear possible, standing all the way and keeping your cadence at 50 rpm or more. Do about 10 of these climbs, with at least a five-mile warmup and cooldown.

If you're short on time, a good bike workout is a one-hour "ride as hard as you can" effort. Find the distance you can ride in one hour and time yourself.

Some of my most productive workouts have been on a bicycle ergometer like the TuboTrainer. After starting with a short warmup, I ride in a gear that allows me to crank for 60 seconds at 90 rpm and raise my heart rate to near its maximum level.

At other times, I go hard for 1½ minutes at 90 rpm, back off and spin until the heart rate is back to 110 or 120 beats per minute, and then go hard again.

The best possible set-up I know of — and I have used it often — is to strap on a heart monitor to register heart rate and wear stereo headphones. The music relieves the boredom and the heart monitor tells me when I have gone above or below my target heart rate. I can often do workouts like this for several hours, as long as the music is to my liking, of course.

Instead of doing intervals on some ergometer workouts, I ride for a long time at steady cadence, usually 75 to 80 rpm. The idea is to sustain the heart rate as long as possible and as evenly as possible, keeping the rpm constant and using gear tension to control heart rate. If, at 75 rpm, the heart goes above target, I ease off the tension by shifting into an easier gear. If it is below the target, I shift into a harder gear.

Training sessions indoors are a good time for heat training. Put on extra layers of clothing to raise your body temperature. Fill your water bottle and drink frequently to maintain your body's built-in radiator. The odometer is insignificant on the stationary bike workout; you should judge the duration of your workout by your heart rate and your watch.

Category 3: Plenty of Tempo (POT)

Plenty of Tempo, otherwise called race pace work, is accomplished during time trials and occasionally by entering less demanding triathlons or single-sport races. Category 3 workouts fit the previous two workout components to an actual situation. Over the long term, they serve as a reliable indicator of your improvement and capabilities. Benefits:

1) Improves race form.

2) Increases pace recognition.

3) Encourages monitoring of heart rate to indicate effort and determine race pace.

The time trial reveals improvement — or lack of it — during your training program. It would be nice to measure blood glycogen, enzyme and hemoglobin levels daily (as do the East German and Russian athletes) to determine the duration and intensity of the next workout, but the athlete's stopwatch and his own sensation of effort can be equally good indicators of overall condition.

Be a clock watcher. On days that require intense work, keep track of splits and total times and compare them with previous weeks. If your times do not improve in a logical progression, allowing for the ratchet action of training, you may have to re-evaluate your training program.

The time trial also helps the athlete dig deeper than he normally would in a workout because the stopwatch is his unrelenting opponent. Time-trialing forces you to focus on the task at hand and eliminate peripheral thoughts and diversions.

Swim: Do 200- to 400-meter intervals in the pool at race pace with about a 30-second rest between sets. An occasional one- or two-mile time trial in the pool or ocean will help test your strength and stamina.

Swim/Ride: The swim/ride workout familiarizes you not only with blood pooling, but also with quick clothing changes when you are cold from swimming. The workout gives you some idea of how long you need to warm up and feel strong on the ride.

Ride/Run: Many a runner fools himself into thinking that the 7:00-minute miles he can crank out in a regular marathon will happen from memory at the end of a long triathlon, but they won't. Regardless of the number of miles you've put in on the roads or at the track, triathlon running is a new experience, resulting from the effect that riding has on the leg muscles.

Toward the latter stages of my triathlon training for the Ironman, I made it a rule never to run unless I had ridden at least 20 miles on the bike. This procedure ensured that I wouldn't go out and run garbage mileage — miles run just to get the maximum weekly mileage figures I had set as a goal. With practice, the transition from riding to running will become the most natural feeling in the world.

I discovered that my most valuable workout was a long ride and a medium-long run. I would go 100 miles in a time trial with only water to drink — no food or electrolytes. Afterward, I would run as many as 10 miles, which, I was surprised to find, I could do without great effort. This workout requires the most recovery time before another one — in my case two days.

THE FOUR-PHASE PLAN TO PEAK PERFORMANCE

Rather than taking a haphazard approach to your competition, why not plan your training strategy for the race? I break my workouts into four phases: Base, Buildup, Peak and Taper. The duration depends on what type of triathlon I'm training for. You will see two figures (weeks of training) on the following phase plans, next to *Duration.* The first figure refers to a USTS-type triathlon, the second figure to an Ironman-type triathlon. The longer the race, the more time you should spend preparing for it. Each phase calls for a particular type of workout category, as previously described.

Note that the Taper is considered a training phase, even though you are not really working out. Its importance, however, cannot be underestimated, so I have given it Phase 4 status. Think of the Taper as the icing on the cake.

Phase 1: The Base

Workouts: Category 1
Duration: 6 to 12 weeks
Goal: Reach 75 percent of aerobic fitness potential

Your first few weeks or months of serious training should be spent building a base. Do Category 1 workouts and emphasize long, steady miles. Necessary equipment should be purchased before beginning serious training. If you're not a cyclist, this is the time to shape up those "glutes." If you're not a swimmer, this is the time to get used to lap swimming. And if you're not a runner, the base workouts will see you through the initial flurry of minor overuse injuries common to beginners.

Phase 2: The Buildup

Workouts: Category 1 and 2
Duration: 6 to 12 weeks
Goal: Reach 90 percent of aerobic fitness potential

Much of your training in the buildup is for sharpening and strengthening, with increasing emphasis on Category 2 interval workouts. Use your stopwatch and heart rate to measure intensity of workouts. Avoid getting dragged down by garbage mileage, a syndrome that worsens as you get stronger and grab for more. Remember that at this phase you need quality work and quality rest. As you gradually increase duration and intensity, base your workouts and weekly load on your ability to recover.

By the end of this phase, you should be doing more Category 2 than Category 1 workouts. Your level of fitness should be at or near 90 percent, at which time you need to back off slightly on your training to 60 or 70 percent during the last two to three weeks of Phase 2. The rest will prepare you for Phase 3.

Guidelines for Recovery

Your guidelines for recovery between hard workouts are as follows:

A. It is generally easier to recover from a swimming workout. Running takes the longest.

B. Resting pulse should be used to determine recovery. Remember: If resting pulse upon awakening is seven or more beats above normal, take it easy or take the day off.

C. Recovery is more important after strength workouts and maximum efforts.

D. Treat each minor injury as potentially major and back off.

E. Warm up, spin, stretch, walk and cool down.

F. If, 10 or 15 minutes into a hard workout, you find you are flat, go home and rest. Do not make it a garbage mileage workout.

G. Drink lots of fluid during and after workouts. Water is a key building block and helps flush the system of wastes. Do not drink alcohol right after a long, fat-burning workout.

H. Do not nap right after major efforts. Stay mildly active with a sedentary pursuit. Napping invites "rigor mortis."

I. Maintain a journal or log so that you can base future training on the recovery rates that will emerge through trial and error.

J. Rest is not your enemy — it is your ally.

Phase 3: Peaking

Workouts: Category 2 and 3
Duration: 3 to 5 weeks
Goal: Reach 100 percent aerobic fitness potential

The final six weeks before a major competition is for fine-tuning, with intensity of work taking precedence over other factors. By now you will have a strong base and aerobic conditioning will be at or near maximum. You are at the point on the Health vs. Fitness Chart where the workout demands on the body are so great that resistance to illness and injury are lowered. Rest and recovery between workouts is imperative.

The workouts should be a mix of Category 3 and 2, with emphasis on time-trialing at medium to long distances. Weekly mileage should drop slightly to allow for both recovery and greater intensity. Don't commit a peaking blunder and peak a week or two too early. When in doubt, back off.

Begin planning the race in your mind, rehearse tactics (like clothing changes) and visualize the competition. To get psyched, I encourage entering a shorter single-sport race two weeks before the major competition.

Phase 4: Taper

Workouts: Category 1
Duration: 3 days to 2 weeks
Goal: Rest to gain 100 percent health and 100 percent fitness

A well-planned taper allows the body to summon all of its reserves for the competition it's about to face. Short races might require only a few days of taper beforehand, but longer races definitely require a longer taper. Too many good athletes, out of fear of losing condition, have trained hard right up to a day or two before a major meet, only to produce mediocre results. But it takes less effort to maintain a level of good condition than it does to achieve it. The taper also allows energy stores to build up fully and the aches and pains of training are given a well-deserved chance to disappear. I rested for a week before the Ironman, doing Category 1 workouts of short duration at an easy pace. The day prior to the week-long rest, I went on a long, hard ride.

Some triathletes have tapered a full two weeks before an Ironman-type triathlon, with good results. Kim Bushong is one of the elite triathletes who prefers long tapers. He goes into serious television training, which involves sitting in front of the tube all day and relaxing.

Insufficient tapering is worse than too much. Athletes fear they will lose all those months of intense training if they rest before the big race. A week of easy workouts won't hurt you, but it might make that race you've trained months for seem less of a challenge than you'd expected.

Here's how your four-phase plan looks on a Health vs. Fitness Chart:

Fig. 4.

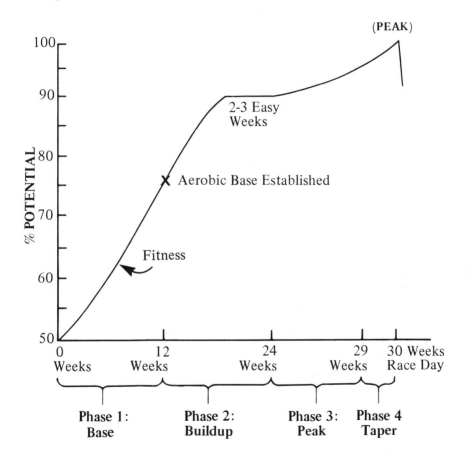

PHASE 1 — BASE: Category 1 workouts until 75 percent fitness reached.

PHASE 2 — BUILDUP: Category 1 and 2 workouts. When 90 percent fitness is reached, back off to 60 percent of mileage.

PHASE 3 — PEAK: Category 3 and Category 2 workouts.

PHASE 4 — TAPER: Category 1 workouts and rest.

7

In Sickness and in Health

Physical fitness is often a cruel mistress. You might say that when you take the vow to achieve and maintain good health that you accept the old axiom, "in sickness and in health." There have been occasions on my way to cardiovascular euphoria that I wondered if I shouldn't give up sports altogether. At any one time, I've had a sore foot, a cold, mental fatigue, loss of appetite and insomnia. It reminds me of the plight of Indiana Jones (*"Raiders of the Lost Ark"*) as he searched the African cave for a rare gold amulet. At every turn, he was faced with unseen death traps. Whereas Jones managed to avoid the poison arrows and 10-ton boulders, I have been flattened by every training pitfall and I made the Dean's List at the School of Hard Knocks.

One piece of wisdom I'll reveal right now is that health comes from more than just proper training. A healthy lifestyle, adequate diet and knowledge of the treatment of injuries is equally important.

As I began to spend more time preparing for the triathlon, three things happened: My social life went to hell, my food bill went through the roof and I found that I began to know more about the treatment of my own overuse injuries than most doctors.

The following section presents some often-heard questions from triathletes about daily living, diet and injury. I've got some answers and some suggestions, but remember that what works for me might not work for you.

DAY-TO-DAY LIVING

I work at a full-time desk job. Will I have time to train for a triathlon?

Yes. If you are already an endurance athlete, you know that you can train with but a few inconveniences, unless you are an elite triathlete like Dave Scott, who sometimes trains all day. Triathlon training is a question of degree. How serious are you? If you're interested in competing at a low level, you can train less than if you are intent on doing well. When I was in serious training for the marathon, I spent 11 or 12 hours a week on the roads. If you're serious about triathloning, you'll have to spend at least 15 hours a week training. I'm not suggesting that you should divide your time this way, but your schedule might look like this: swim two hours (4320 yards), cycle eight hours (150 miles) and run five hours (40 miles). In my opinion, this is the minimum amount of training necessary to complete the tougher Ironman-type triathlons.

If you're interested in completing a USTS-type triathlon, which requires about three hours, you can still do well on less training, say 10 hours a week. The number of hours you spend working out depends a lot on your background in sports. If you're an experienced endurance athlete who can swim a mile, you could finish a short triathlon with minimum training. But if you've never run a step in your life and are out of shape, plan to train for six months before entering a triathlon.

When is the best time of day to work out?

It usually depends on how you arrange your daily work schedule. I often worked eight-hour days, even while training for the Ironman, so I would have two very hard workouts on the weekend and one other on a weekday afternoon or evening. Some people prefer to train in the morning when the air is clean and traffic is light, while others who find that their bodies don't respond well until later in the day train during the lunch hour or after work. The best time of day to train is when your body is at its peak energy level, thus allowing you to gain the most from your workout.

How do I stay psyched for my training?

I make it a point to remind myself every morning when I get out of bed that I have a goal. You might post a calendar with the date of the big race circled in red. Share your excitement and goals with friends, but don't be a bore. Remind them that your training will pay off on race day. Read stories about the triathlon. Review your training diary frequently. Support from a spouse or roommate is important. You are responsible for getting him or her involved in your training and the anticipation of the race. Do so in such a way that your friend understands what you are going through and enjoys helping. Many triathletes combine their big race with a vacation and bring along that special, supportive person.

Sometimes I have to miss a workout because of a business or family commitment. Should I train doubly hard the next day?

No, but I used to do that before I got wise. You might feel guilty if you miss a workout and associate it with weakness. Missing one day — even two or three days — won't hurt your general condition. In this situation, rearrange your workout schedule for the next several days, keeping in mind the hard/ easy training formula.

Once you are an experienced endurance athlete, maintaining fitness requires less time because the cardiovascular/aerobic base is already there. Many triathletes are veteran endurance athletes who spend little time training — 10 hours or less a week — and yet they complete triathlons without difficulty. Remember, though, that their goal is *completing* the triathlon, not *racing* the triathlon.

While I'm in training, do I say goodbye to the nightlife?

It depends on your outlook on life. There are two camps: I fall into the "enjoy life to its fullest" camp. Other triathletes hold down the "avoid stress at all costs" camp. Some nights, I'll admit, I'm so wasted after a long, hard workout that I'll eat dinner and go right to bed. I used to have what I called a "fry factor." When I was fried to a crisp, I was good for nothing more than sleeping. But at other times, I don't hesitate to paint the town red after a light training day. Some triathletes can train hard, party all night and a day later be ready for another hard workout and more partying. You've got to know the limitations of your body. I don't advocate going out every night, but I will do it once or twice a week. It's my time to unwind mentally.

What do I do the night before a triathlon?

Here's what I do on the eve of the triathlon: I get my gear ready early in the day, double-check everything, look over the course — if I haven't already — and then go out to dinner. I'll have dinner with a few friends, and a beer or two to relieve pre-race jitters. Then before I go to bed I drink two or three glasses of water to assure proper hydration.

Don't count on getting a lot of sleep the night before the big race. Do that two days before the race. If your race is on Saturday morning, get plenty of rest on Thursday night.

What do I do on the morning of the race?

Get up early enough to allow time to 1) eat breakfast, if any; 2) drink fluids; 3) use the bathroom (allow time for standing in line!); 4) check out gear one more time; and 5) warm up, which includes getting into the water and splashing around. Allow enough time to do all of this without being rushed.

How can I monitor my health?

Some athletes swear by pulse monitoring. They take their pulse every morning before getting out of bed, and once an average is established, they can detect overtraining or impending illness by an elevated pulse, say 10 beats a minute. If your heart rate rises by that much, you should probably back off on your training. Your mental state is also a good tipoff to your general health. Overtraining often results in irritability, loss of motivation, apathy and rapid shifts in mood. It can also disturb your sleep and lead to a loss of appetite and weight.

From what I've read here, won't I need more sleep with the extra training time required?

Yes. The additional time you spend training means that you'll need more rest, some of it in the form of sleep. If you need eight hours of sleep now, you may need as many as nine or 10 hours as your training increases. And it should be sound sleep.

DIET AND NUTRITION

What do I eat while training?

I'm not going to plan your meals, but in doing so, you should keep in mind some rules about nutrition. We are a "man-machine." Food is the man-machine's fuel — and raw ingredients for building and repairing, which go on around the clock. The fuel is composed of three basic ingredients: carbohydrates, fat and protein. As you know, the higher the octane of the gasoline your car uses, the more efficiently your engine runs; you get more miles from a gallon of gas. The same goes for different types of food. High-octane food is high in carbohydrates, low in fat and protein. While fat may be produced from carbohydrate, excess protein and dietary fat, neither fat nor protein can produce carbohydrate in noticeable amounts with the same facility. Carbohydrate is converted into glucose, which in turn is metabolized into glycogen and stored in the muscles where it is ready to be summoned during exercise. The well-trained athlete can hold about 600 grams of glycogen in his muscles (2700 calories). Even if you make every attempt to resupply your body with glucose, you will burn off all that glycogen before the end of most endurance events. But never fear. Fat and protein are both sources of fuel, even though the untrained body has as much difficulty turning them into glucose as an oil refinery does turning sludge into gas. And that's true despite the fact that gram for gram, fat has more than twice the energy of carbohydrate (one fat gram equals 9.3 calories). Covert Bailey, in his book *Fit or Fat*, makes a good analogy between carbos and fat. Carbos are tinder to start a fire — they burn quickly but don't give off much heat. Fat is the log — it burns slowly and gives off plenty of heat. The only way to improve utilization of those fat stores is to train your body, and that occurs through intense, long workouts that exhaust your glycogen stores. Just as you train to improve your performance, the body trains itself to convert those fats.

If you eat the typical American diet, you're getting too much fat and too little carbohydrate. The less fat on your body, the less weight you have to carry around and the faster you'll be. The breakdown between carbohydrate, fat and protein for the athlete should be as follows: carbo 75 percent, fat 15 percent, protein 10 percent. Most American diets are divided more evenly among the three. Since you're in training, you might think you need more protein, but you don't. The 60 grams you need every day is provided in a diet with 10 percent protein.

If you're wondering how many calories to munch down in a day, you can start with 3000 and go as high as 6000 — not a lot when you consider you burn as many as 800 to 1000 calories for every hour of training.

By carbohydrates do you mean cake and ice cream?

Yes and no. Sweets are called simple carbohydrates. They're like jet fuel — powerful but quick-burning. When you sit down for a meal, you should concentrate on complex carbohydrates, which include pasta, bread, rice, potatoes and cereal grains.

Most complex-carbohydrate foods are also high in essential vitamins and minerals. Save the dessert for after-dinner snacks.

I follow a simple rule when it comes to raiding the icebox: Eat what the body craves (not what the body is addicted to). When the body craves a particular food, it is probably lacking some mineral, vitamin or nutrient.

If I taper for a race and load up on "carbos," won't I gain weight?

Yes, but it won't amount to more than a pound or two. And the added weight is mostly water stored with the carbohydrates, which is necessary for them to burn efficiently. A few extra pounds is a desirable side effect of carbohydrate loading, and the extra weight is quickly lost in the race as sweat.

What are the caloric costs of running, cycling and swimming?

First, understand that the body burns calories 24 hours a day; even sleeping burns about 65 calories per hour. Also, the number of calories an individual burns during exercise depends on sex, body weight and intensity of training. Here is a comparison of how body weight influences running: A 120-pound runner training at 7:20 pace will burn 80 calories per mile, while a 200-pound runner will burn 131 calories per mile.

Now compare the number of calories burned according to pace: The 120-pound runner going at 7:20 pace will burn 10.9 calories per minute, but if he increases his pace to 7:00; he will burn 13.8 calories per minute. Here is the caloric cost of the three sports:

CALORIC COST OF SWIMMING, CYCLING AND RUNNING

Hourly Rate

SWIM

11:00 / 220 yards	300
5:30 / 220 yards	600

BIKE

6:00 / mile (10 mph)	415
3:00 / mile (20 mph)	850+

RUN

8:00 / mile	690
6:40 / mile	850+

A fallacy of comparing calories burned during exercise with calories consumed is that many people neglect to account for calorie burnoff from everyday living, which adds up to about 2000 calories for the average-size person. In addition, the basal metabolism remains at a high level for several hours after exercise, accounting for further calorie burnoff. In other words, the stove takes a while to cool after you turn it off.

What is carbohydrate-loading?

This buzz word was the biggest thing in sports several years ago, but now it's well known. It simply means that you eat more foods high in complex carbohydrates. Begin carbohydrate-loading several days before a competition and continue until the eve of the race. Go strictly for carbos and consume few high-protein foods and fats.

When carbohydrate-loading first gained popularity, it was preceded by a three-day depletion phase, during which you ate only protein-rich foods and few — or no — carbohydrates. Scientists discovered, however, that this phase placed more stress on the body and had so slight an effect in the body's additional ability to store more carbos that most no longer recommend it.

What should I eat the day prior to the race?

Eat a big breakfast, concentrating on a low-sugar cereal, pancakes, French toast, fruit juice and coffee — if you drink it. For lunch you might have potatoes, rice or pasta and plenty of water. For dinner, plan a meal high in carbos. Spaghetti is a favorite of mine. I do not recommend Mexican dinners or pizza as both are high in fat (from the cheese). Don't experiment; eat what agrees with you.

Just to give you an idea of how bizarre prerace dinners can get, I went to one before the San Francisco Marathon in 1978 where I drank four beers and ate a half-gallon of chocolate ice cream and a pound of frozen peas. The beers relaxed me, the ice cream provided the carbos and the peas cleaned me out the next morning. I ran a 2:21 and felt great throughout the race.

Some athletes prefer to eat an early breakfast, depending on when the triathlon begins and how short it is. Others like to compete on an empty stomach. Whatever your preference, just don't drink a high-sugar drink one hour or less before the race. The sugar enters the bloodstream, stimulating the release of insulin from the pancreas and reducing the amount of glucose normally released from the liver. The result: Your body is robbed of a valuable source of energy — blood glucose. In other words, you become hypoglycemic.

Dr. David Costill, director of the Human Performance Labs at Ball State University in Muncie, Indiana, has tested athletes who drink a high-sugar drink before exercising, and his results are clear — it reduces your ability to perform.

Is it true that caffeine can help you in a long race?

Dr. Costill's studies indicate it will. In one study, athletes ingested about 220 milligrams of caffeine (equivalent to two cups of coffee) before two hours of exercise. The result was a 7 percent increase in the amount of work they could perform. Caffeine assists in the metabolization of fats for fuel, stimulates the central nervous system and increases the heart's force of contraction. The use of caffeine by athletes is nothing new: Frank Shorter drank de-fizzed Coca-Cola (very high in caffeine) in his Olympic marathon races. Although caffeine has some potential benefits, it also has some side effects. For one thing, it's a diuretic, and some people who drink liquids high in caffeine get upset stomachs.

How about vitamin and mineral supplements?

Bill Rodgers probably has the most reasonable attitude toward vitamins and minerals. The former American-record holder in the marathon says that he takes a multiple vitamin with his breakfast for cheap insurance.

Other athletes vitamin-load. There are two schools of thought on the subject: those who believe that all vitamins give you is expensive urine and those who believe that the stress of training depletes the body of vitamins and minerals at a greatly elevated rate. For what it's worth, in training for my first Ironman, I took no vitamins and had four colds in the two months prior to the race. I also overtrained. The next year, I took megadoses of vitamins (25 grams of vitamin C daily along with 50 other pills) and had no colds or related problems. But I had a vitamin bill of $180 a month. Unless you're under the care of a nutritionist, however, I don't recommend this; there are potential dangers with vitamin-loading.

What should I eat and drink during the triathlon?

Fluid intake is more crucial than food consumption, and a lot easier. In general, eating is recommended only during a long triathlon. How much liquid you consume is directly proportional to the weather and your body weight. You need to drink

DEHYDRATION DISTANCES								
Temp.	**6:00/mile**			**8:00/mile**			**10:00/mile**		
	1%	**3%**	**8%**	**1%**	**3%**	**8%**	**1%**	**3%**	**8%**
50°F	9	26	60+	30	60+	60+	36	60+	60+
55	7	20	55	17	50	60+	36	60+	60+
60	6	17	45	11	32	60+	36	60+	60+
65	5	14	38	8	24	60+	18	55	60+
70	4	13	34	6	19	50	11	33	60+
75	4	11	30	5	16	42	8	24	60+
80	3	10	27	5	14	37	7	20	50
85	3	9	25	4	12	32	5	15	41
90	3	9	23	4	11	28	5	13	36
95	3	8	21	3	10	26	4	12	31
100	2	7	19	3	9	23	4	10	28
105	2	7	18	3	8	21	3	9	25
110	2	6	17	2	7	20	3	8	22
115	2	6	16	2	7	18	3	8	21
120	2	6	15	2	6	17	2	7	19

The figures in the three columns represent the distances covered by a runner without fluid replacement, which will result in weight losses of 1 percent, 3 percent and 8 percent. A weight loss of 1 percent represents the distance at which Dr. David Costill recommends the runner should have started fluid replacement. A weight loss of 3 percent represents the distance at which the running performance may be impaired if fluid replacement has not been utilized. A weight loss of 8 percent represents extreme dehydration and one should not anticipate exceeding these distances without fluid replacement.

whatever it takes to avoid losing 2 percent or more of your body weight during competition. On a hot day, that might mean six or more pints of water.

I have a crude formula: If you don't need to urinate during the race, you certainly aren't overhydrated and you might even be getting dehydrated. There is little room for error when it comes to dehydration. A 3 percent weight loss will hinder performance, and an 8 percent loss can cause extreme dehydration, and possible heat stroke.

It's no secret that electrolyte drinks like ERG, which contain glucose and some trace minerals, offer more than water. However, some people can't stand the taste of electrolyte drinks or digest them without getting an upset stomach. Before trying electrolyte drinks in competition, you should experiment with them during training rides. I prefer apple or some non-acidic fruit juice during both workouts and competitions, but water is still the big favorite among most triathletes. A few drink soda pop or tea.

I follow these general principles during a race:

Swim: Most triathlon swims are too short to require liquid intake, but you should note that you do "sweat" during the swim. It is possible to drink and even eat while swimming. Three-time winner of the Escape From Alcatraz Triathlon, Dave Horning, ate a banana while floating on his back during a 30-mile swim around New York's Manhattan Island.

Try to avoid swallowing saltwater. Not only is it a diuretic, but it can cause an upset stomach.

Bike: This is the best time in the race to eat and drink. You needn't worry about getting cramps or an upset stomach, because of the smooth motion of pedaling. In a short, hot-weather triathlon, you should drink about two bottles of water. Food is optional, but bananas do go down well. In a medium-length triathlon, you might need as many as six bottles of water (96 ounces) and a couple of bananas. In a warm-weather triathlon of four hours or more, you should drink as much as 16 ounces of water every 10 or 15 miles. I also like to eat bananas and fig bars. High-carbohydrate foods like these are recommended for their ease of digestion. High-fat foods like peanut butter and bacon-bit sandwiches are definitely out.

Run: It is during the last stage of the triathlon (usually the run) that you need energy the most, but, ironically, it's also the worst time to ingest food. Eating is almost out of the question and drinking is difficult. Whatever you do at this stage, don't experiment. Scott Tinley and several other elite triathletes tried a corn-syrup solution they weren't familiar with during the October 1982 Ironman, and they regretted it when they got sick. Unfortunately, they were engaged in an experimental program and had no choice in what they ate or drank that day.

Whether or not you increase your intake of sugar is a personal decision. Dave Scott drank only water and ate nothing but bananas in the October 1982 Ironman, while veteran ultramarathoner Tom Osler drinks fluids that are extremely high in sugar.

What about beer and wine? Can I drink it?

During a race or workout, I don't recommend it. After a workout, though, I occasionally have a beer. Attitudes have changed in the last decade concerning alcohol consumption by athletes, and although scientific research has revealed little in the way of its effect on performance, a beer once in a while won't harm you. Social attitudes, more than anything, have determined the athlete's consumption of alcohol. Marty Liquori, runner and TV sports commentator, told the press that he liked to hit the town before a race and have a few beers, a statement that almost got him kicked off the 1968 Olympic team. A decade later, when Dr. George Sheehan proclaimed that beer-drinking is pleasurable and harmless, beer sales to runners soared. The best-selling author went so far as to drink while competing, downing a six-pack one year in the Boston Marathon. He has good reason, too: Beer is high in complex car-bohydrates and a relaxant. On the other hand, it is a mild di-uretic and has been linked with a reduction in heat stress re-sistance. Sheehan isn't alone in his alcohol consumption habit, either. A lot of cyclists who compete in the Tour de France drink wine every night between races.

I'm not against drinking in moderation, but bear in mind that athletes are not immune to alcoholism.

INJURY

Now that I'm training for three different sports, can I expect to have more injuries?

That depends on your sport of origin. Runners definitely should have fewer overuse injuries from running as they spend less time pounding the roads and more time swimming and cy-cling. Swimmers, cyclists and other athletes might find that they have more injuries as they increase their running mileage. Overuse injuries are the triathlete's main concern – that and getting run over by a Mack truck. I think these are the biggest risks in the three sports: swimming – colds and sore shoulders; cycling – crashing; running – sore legs and feet.

Could you be more specific about what injuries I may en-counter?

Run: Achilles tendinitis, sore calf muscles, sore or pulled ham-strings; shinsplints (sore shins); sciatica (usually in the form of hip pain); plantar fasciitis (sore arch); bone bruise (usually on the heel); inflamed ligaments and tendons; stress fractures in the leg and foot; athlete's foot; chondromalacia (sore knee). And I've probably left out a half-dozen other problems.

Causes: 1) overtraining; 2) inferior running shoes; 3) muscle weakness and instability; 4) biomechanical abnormalities in footstrike; 5) limb length difference (one leg longer than the other); 6) poor hygiene.

Bike: chondromalacia, numb hands, numb butt, numb feet, numb private parts, sore neck, sore back, broken bones, scrapes and bruises, bee stings, boils, sunburn, windburn.

Causes: 1) crashing; 2) nerve irritations; 3) overuse; 4) improper seat height and stem length; 5) bees.

Swim: infected ear, shoulder and elbow bursitis, eye infection, stings.

Causes: 1) dirty water; 2) overuse; 3) poor technique; 4) sea life.

How do I deal with an injury and how do I know if it calls for backing off from training?

Deal with every pain or injury as though it were major. Probe, test and concentrate on the possible causes of your injury; don't shrug it off and continue to train, thinking you can tough it out.

Generally, if pain increases as the workout progresses, you should discontinue training. If the pain decreases as you proceed with a workout, the injury is probably minor, but monitor it closely anyway. When I am backing off from an injury, or recovering from one, I train until the pain starts, and then I stop. Any pain that lasts for more than one week or worsens with time or during a workout should be brought to the attention of the appropriate medical specialist, preferably someone who knows about sportsmedicine. Being cautious and backing off a few days is a far safer strategy than taking the risk of continuing your training and winding up injured for a much longer time.

The beauty of the triathlon is that even while you are injured, you can lay off one sport for a while and concentrate on the other two. Except for colds, flu or major conflagrations, you should not have long periods of down time because of injury.

Injury, however, is something we all live with. As runner-writer Joe Henderson once said, there's a certain amount of pain coursing through our bodies all the time; it's just that sometimes it's concentrated in one place.

I've heard horror stories about chondromalacia. What is it and what causes it?

Chondromalacia is a wastebasket term physicians use for a sore knee. Although overuse is the main cause, chondromalacia can result from a biomechanical abnormality, usually in the feet.

The knee is a complex joint surrounded by ligaments and tendons. In between the ligaments and tendons are bursae, sacs of fluid that help lubricate the joint. Riding on a thin cushion of synovial fluid and covering the joint is the patella, or kneecap. When the kneecap is forced to ride out of its natural groove, either through biomechanical causes or from inflammation caused by overuse, the knee is painful to bend. Often you will notice a clicking sound from the knee as it is moved. Chondromalacia can be bad enough to make running impossible, and cycling — even climbing stairs — painful. The condition usually takes between two and four weeks to go away. Treatment includes rest, icing the knee to reduce inflammation and correcting any biomechanical abnormalities in the foot.

What is "swimmer's ear"?

Swimmer's ear is caused by bacteria that invade the outer ear and cause infection. It usually occurs in young people, but it does not always discriminate with age. Two causes are a dirty pool and inadequate evacuation of water from the ear. Symptoms include fever, dizziness, loss of balance and difficulty in hearing. Antibiotics are effective.

Can I continue to run with a stress fracture?

No. Stop training and see your orthopedist or podiatrist. Stress fractures occur more frequently in women than they do in men. The main cause is overuse, the result of doing too much in too short a time. Swimming, and sometimes cycling, are usually possible,

Is it possible to continue training with minor scrapes and bruises incurred in a crash?

Yes. A few scrapes and bruises shouldn't prevent you from sticking to your normal training pace, but be sure the wounds are kept clean. Flush them daily with soap and water, soaking them in hot water to increase blood circulation and speed healing. Keep the scrapes covered with gauze to protect them from road grime.

Can I train while I have a cold?

A cold is often a sign of overtraining, and it might be a cue to curtail or cut back on your training. If you don't have a fever, you can probably work out, but with less intensity than normal. If you've got the flu, crawl back into bed, take two aspirin and drink plenty of liquids.

What is the standard self-treatment for the typical overuse injury?

Remember this acronym: HIRT. It stands for Heat, Ice, Rest and Time. When the injury occurs, ice it frequently during the first 48 hours to reduce inflammation. Ice it for 15 minutes at a time or until the skin becomes red and numb; icing for longer periods will not yield better results. After 48 hours, alternate applying heat and cold to the injured area. Heat increases blood flow. Follow a hot soak or compress application with more icing to reduce inflammation. Rest is also necessary to heal the injury. Don't try to be a Duke or Bogey and train through the pain. It takes time to heal an overuse injury, so HIRT don't HURT.

Sometimes I get cramps in my legs. What causes them and how can they be prevented?

Cramps occur most frequently in the calves or hamstrings, and afflict the untrained athlete more often. They're not unheard of in the highly trained athlete, however, in which case they are called "professional cramps."

An unconditioned muscle, which is unable to rid itself of lactic acid as quickly as it builds up, has a lower threshold for work than a trained muscle. When it can no longer function at an elevated level, it becomes fatigued and can go into spasm. The elite athlete, even though his muscles are well-conditioned, still has a threshold beyond which a muscle can't perform, and when that threshold is reached, a cramp can ensue. At the October 1982 Ironman, Dave Scott said he was pushed to his limit in the swim by Mark Allen. During the bike race, one of his hamstrings cramped, a good indication that he exceeded his muscle threshold during the swim.

Cramping can also be the result of dehydration. If you feel a cramp coming on, drink liquids. After the cramp has struck, treatment consists of massage, rest and static stretching. If you cramp during a race, you have two options: continue at full speed and hope that it will go away, or slow down and give the muscle a chance to rest and rid itself of excess lactic acid.

Can you "hit the wall" in cycling and swimming as you can in running?

Yes. It's called "the bonk" in cycling lingo and "the bear" in swimming. Ed Burke, a well-known physiologist among bicycle racers, writes in *Inside the Cyclist* that the bonk is caused by six factors: 1) lack of blood glucose; 2) lack of fluid; 3) loss of minerals or electrolytes; 4) overheating; 5) depletion of muscle fuels; and 6) increased lactic acid levels. Traditionally, the wall has been associated with the 21-mile mark in the marathon. The bonk can occur as early as 30 miles into a ride. You bonk or hit the wall when the body runs out of complex carbohydrates and starts to burn fats more predominantly. One of the primary goals of training is to avoid the bonk, the wall or the bear by developing efficient alternative energy systems (fat burning).

How important is the warmup and warmdown in workouts and competition?

You don't have to spend hours warming up or warming down, but both should become a part of your training routine. In competition, warming up becomes less important as the distance of the event increases and, in a long event, you can warm up during the early stages of the race. There's no sense in wasting energy warming up for a long race.

Before a run, stretching reduces the chances of injury from a pulled muscle. Concentrate on the Achilles tendons, the hamstrings, the quadriceps and calves, the shoulders and the back. Stretching is not quite as important in the bike ride or the swim; my warmup during a workout usually consists of working up gradually to a harder effort.

The warmdown generally consists of working out at a less intense level before quitting. The duration should be directly proportional to the length of your workout. If you have been out on a six-hour bike ride, I wouldn't advise plopping down on the sofa immediately after walking through your door. Your body needs time to unwind, so you should spin easily for a mile or two, shower, drink and then do something that will keep you mildly active or at least alert for the next several hours.

Why do many triathletes shave their legs?

The benefits gained from shaving legs and other body hair are primarily psychological. Shaved legs have greater tactile sensitivity. As you cycle along and air rushes over your hairless legs, you get a sensation of speed, although the streamline effect is negligible. Some swimmers shave their bodies entirely — down to the eyebrows — before an important competition. Top triathlete Kim Bushong, however, prefers to leave his arms unshaved. He says that during the swim, shaved arms feel as though they have less drag and, as a result, less ability to pull you through the water.

Professional cyclists shave their legs because they always receive a massage after a race, and shaved legs facilitate massage. Treatment of minor scrapes is also less of a hassle with shaved legs.

It seems that everybody dresses differently when they train. Is there a right way?

The amount and type of clothing you wear depends on your body's ability to withstand cold and heat. No two bodies are alike. Some athletes can't stand the cold; others can't handle the heat.

But there are general guidelines that you should adhere to. First, cold weather:

1) Dress in several layers. Air trapped between layers acts as insulation.

2) Wear wool or the new polypropyl material. Wool and polypropyl wick away moisture but retain heat.

3) Always overdress, especially for cycling. You can take off clothing when you warm up, but you can't add on as easily if you get cold.

4) When cycling, take extra care with the hands and feet. "Booties," which slip over cycling shoes, help keep your feet warmer in very cold weather.

5) Protect the knees. They have little insulation (fat), and the blood vessels are close to the skin. Cover them with sweat pants or cycling tights to keep them warm. You can tell if your knees need warming when the skin around them turns red on a cold day, or if they ache.

6) Cover the head. About 40 percent of your body heat is lost through the head.

Rules for hot weather:

1) Wear white or reflective clothing.

2) Wear a hat and/or something to shade the eyes.

3) Apply suntan lotion if you anticipate being outside for long hours, even if it's cloudy.

4) Avoid getting your running shoes wet from water dousings; they're heavier and can cause blisters.

HEAT SAFETY INDEX

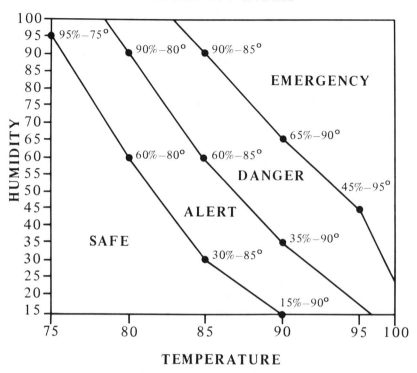

TEMPERATURE

The chart is adapted from the Weather Service Operations Manual. "Safe" temperature-humidity readings generally allow for normal activity. "Alert" conditions require caution during long, hard runs. "Danger" levels may demand a reduction of training. Strenuous cycling or running is not recommended during "Emergency" conditions.

I plan to enter a triathlon that has a swim in very cold water. Right now I have low body fat. Should I increase it through diet?

No. Resistance to hypothermia is not always determined by body fat. Just as some runners perform better than others in heat, so do some swimmers perform better than others in cold water. Your best strategy would be to train in cold water as much as possible before the race to build tolerance.

Can a massage before a race improve performance?

I can't recommend having a massage right before a race, unless it is strictly for relaxation and is nothing more than light stroking. Deep tissue massage or any other vigorous massage is best saved for after the race to speed recovery. A vigorous massage before a race can leave you sore and tired.

Should I take aspirin for minor injuries?

Aspirin reduces inflammation and is a mild analgesic. Many athletes use aspirin and find that it is effective in reducing the aches and pains of minor injuries. You can take two aspirin an hour before a workout with no ill effects. By taking the aspirin before the workout, you will obtain the maximum benefit from its anti-inflammatory properties. I know one triathlete who took six aspirin in the Ironman to relieve painful neuromas in his feet.

Are there stronger drugs that are more effective than aspirin in reducing pain?

Yes, but these drugs are available only by prescription. They have a much greater chance of causing side effects, usually in the form of an upset stomach. Non-steroidal, anti-inflammatory medications include Indocin, Butazolidin, Naprosyn, Motrin and Tolectin. They are not painkillers. Painkilling drugs like codeine are not recommended because they can mask a potentially serious pain. Without your body's natural warning system, you could easily continue training and make the injury worse.

The steroidal drug, cortisone, is one of the most powerful anti-inflammatory drugs known. But it's not a panacea. Although cortisone works quickly and usually with dramatic effects, the injury still needs time and rest on its own to heal properly. Cortisone is recommended only as a last resort. Remember: There are no panaceas when it comes to an injury. In fact, there are many dangers with so-called panaceas. As my grandfather used to say, "God heals and the doctor sends the bill."

8

Mind Games

Dave Scott, 1980 and 1982 winner of the Ironman, said these revealing words about training: "Training for the event is mentally unbelievable. The race is demanding, but I think if you can persevere through the training months you've got it in the bag." Julie Moss said that training for the Ironman was so exhausting, both physically and mentally, that by the time she got to the starting line, she felt a tremendous sense of relief. Is it possible that man's real limitations are in his mind and not his body?

In recent years, athletes, scientists and coaches have sought the answer to this question. Evidence indicates that the successful athlete not only does the right workouts, but also has a superior mental and emotional outlook. As Scott said, the day-to-day grind of training can wear you down. But the effect is more far-reaching than general fatigue. Intensive training can impinge on your social life. It has ruined careers, caused divorces and canceled wedding plans. Awareness of the risks of overtraining is the first step in avoiding its negative effects, which are both physical and mental.

The training triathlete is analogous to a high-performance machine: His body requires attention around the clock. A great deal of mental energy goes into the body-machine to keep it psyched for training. The dedication to go out and train when you're not feeling up to par and the willpower to back off on some good days, has to come from somewhere. There has to be a lot of ego involved, a lot of inward direction, a lot of concentration on yourself. As your training increases, you become the most important person in your life. You will often have days when you wonder whether your narcissism is self-destructive.

Like most athletes, you probably consider training time as just the hours you actually spend exercising. But there is more to it than that. Training time includes the hours in between, the time you spend sitting around beat to a pulp, useless for anything else. It's the extra time you spend sleeping because you're so tired. It's the time you stay home on a Saturday night. This sacrifice can be very draining, and you have to be strong both physically and mentally to take it.

Training does have a bright side, too. There are the times when you are training at such a high level that you feel like the strongest person on the face of the earth; you're invincible and nothing can stand in your way. You might feel that being able to train for six hours a day is just an indication of your ability to go out and party. You can be very gregarious and extroverted at times. It's been my experience that the triathlete in training takes on a Jekyll and Hyde personality — happy one day, depressed the next. I believe that mood shifts are the result of a basic body rhythm or cycle, if you will. I don't believe in biorhythms, per se, or a formula that someone might have developed that can be plugged into a computer. But there are those ups and downs. Recognizing them is crucial, because they will determine how you train. Go with the flow in your training. When you feel good, push. When you feel bad, back off.

When you feel good, write letters to yourself describing how good you feel. Write down what you intend to do, your goals and changes in attitude. During those times when you feel bad, when you feel like quitting, look back on your notes to help you through those inevitable times.

Getting Primed

On a day-to-day basis, depending on what your style is, you have to develop a sense of getting primed for a workout. It may take getting up an hour earlier and just sitting around and preparing — stretching, listening to music, reading a newspaper or magazine, drinking six cups of coffee, visiting the bathroom, whatever. Get a ritual going, especially if you are preparing for a hard workout. The purpose is to summon enough mental energy to get you through your workout. Plan a regular winddown ritual afterward, too — something to look forward to toward the end of the workout. You might spin the last two miles of your bike ride, stretch, read the newspaper, take a hot bath, drink a couple of beers, or watch television.

There's nothing mystical about this mental energy (although triathlon guru Ian Jackson might disagree). Simply call attention to it in your training. Recognize it when you are concentrating, when you are summoning that extra 5 or 10 percent that the normal individual would not have on a mediocre or bad day.

Some days the energy won't be there, especially after five or six days of good training. What frequently follows are three or four days of depression. The first day you go out and have nothing. You say to yourself, "Okay, that's cool. I've just come off four or five days of real hard training. I'll take it easy today." The next day the same thing happens; you have nothing. Whether or not you have it physically (and you probably don't), you just don't feel as though you have it mentally. Sometimes on workouts, I would just feel like crying. I'd ask myself, "What happened to that tremendous positive energy I had just a week ago?"

When this happens, don't panic. Don't think you've lost your good condition. You haven't. When you feel bad, you feel bad for a reason. The cause may be physiological or something subconscious. Back off and rest.

MENTAL TOUGHENING

During competition in the triathlon, especially the races that take four hours or more, you will need to draw on your mental reserves. Training through adversity is the best way I know to get tough. Bill Rodgers claims that the only reason many of the country's best runners hail from his home town of Boston is because of the foul weather they train in. It's either hot and humid or cold and wet. The more adverse your training conditions, the easier it will be when you face hard times in the race.

A favorite workout of mine that draws on mental toughness and creates adversity is a bonk ride followed by a short run. I go out for a 100-mile ride with only water to drink — no food or ERG. Eighty miles into the ride, I've usually bonked and feel totally spent and drained. Simulating race conditions occasionally will help extend your limits. Tailor the hard workout to your own abilities and situation.

I don't believe some athletes have more mental energy than others. There is not the disparity among athletes in capacity to develop mental energy that there is in genetic ability, which determines how strong you can be or how much endurance you

can have. Mental energy comes down to a four-letter word —
guts. Guts and concentration — and whoever can draw most on
that untapped reserve of mental energy winds up the winner.
Dave Scott has argued that swimmers acquire more mental
toughness because they train countless thousands of yards alone
in a swimming pool, a setting that deprives the senses. His contention is that this makes them better triathletes. He might be
right.

DISSOCIATION VS. ASSOCIATION

What do triathletes think about during the race? In a short
race, you will probably be preoccupied with worries about
finding your gear at the next transition area, your position in
relation to others, your nagging injury or mechanical difficul-
ties. In the longer race, however, you have more time to think,
but what about? Should you enjoy the scenery or concentrate
all the time? During the race, endurance athletes fall into two
categories of thought: dissociators and associators. Dissociators
try to take their minds off the race. They are the guys who
count backward from one thousand or design and build a
house in their minds. In general, they are the less competitive
athletes. Associators, on the other hand, concentrate on their
bodies, on what's going on inside them. They constantly monitor their vital signs, their heart rates, their breathing, their
overall position in the race, their stride in the run or their stroke
in the water. They are the truly competitive athletes who are
able to concentrate.

Many successful athletes both associate and dissociate during
a race. Don Kardong, 1976 Olympic marathoner, is a good
example. He describes his mental state during a marathon in
Jim Lilliefors' insightful book, *The Running Mind:* "During the
first 10 miles of the race, I try to dissociate myself from what
I'm doing. I talk, joke and daydream in ways that remove me
from the race. But after 10 miles, my consciousness re-enters
the picture, and concentration begins. From that point on, the
problem is concentration, and the feeling is one of acute association with the task at hand . . ."

One of the most difficult endurance sports — marathon swimming — challenges the athlete's mental strength as much as his
physical strength. During the entire event, he has only his
thoughts to deal with. The only people he sees are race officials
who follow him in boats. Paul Asmuth, winner of the 1980 and
1981 professional marathon four-race series, reflects on the

mental struggle that ensues when physical stamina is no longer enough to maintain constant effort: "Then I start playing these mental games, attaching something from my head to the boat or attaching mechanical arms to my arms to pull them along. But it's a constant, ongoing trick you have to play. Sometimes I break down and find myself crying."

Here's how I apply dissociation/association in the triathlon: I go through the swim as though it were a nice workout, but concentrating on staying in contact with the front pack. On the bike I work really hard to establish my position. I enjoy the scenery during the first part of the ride, all the while keying on individuals ahead and catching up with them. As I pass one rider, I focus on the next one. In the latter stages of the ride, I begin to dig in mentally.

In the run, the real fun begins. I focus on a runner's back and pull myself up to him. There is a definite advantage to being behind: You can concentrate better on your opposition and the guy ahead must break his concentration and rhythm to look back and find out where you are. In the Hawaii Ironman Triathlon, the mental battle is monumental. It takes everything you've got to keep moving, much less key on your competition. Toward the end of the race, I repeat my own special mantra to myself, which consists of these three thoughts: "Focus. Tunnel vision. Concentrate."

PAINKILLERS AND ALTERED STATES

As discussed in Chapter 4, the best painkillers in the world are those produced by the human body. More and more evidence today supports the contention that physical activity speeds the release of these natural chemicals, called endorphins, produced in the brain. Empirically, we can see that greater quantities of these chemicals are found in athletes than sedentary people. Just ask someone who is out of shape how he feels when he exercises and he'll tell you he's in pain within minutes of beginning activity. Consider, too, the times you've been in an accident. If you've ever broken a bone, you know that initially there is little noticeable pain. The body is responding to its nerve signals and sending painkillers to the injury.

The so-called "runner's high," with its euphoric feelings and almost religious experience of oneness with the body, has been attributed to endorphins. All athletes, however, feel the same sensations of a runner's high. Endorphins are released during any prolonged exercise.

The only drawback of endorphins is that they sometimes work too well. It's not uncommon to find yourself feeling better as you increase your training: The more you train, the more endorphins are released. I've had days when I was in a quasi-drunken stupor. The net result of such a pleasant state, however, is overtraining. You want to make the euphoria last, so you keep training hard and eventually may strain an ankle, a knee, or get sick. Conversely, when you stop training for a while, your endorphin level decreases. Despite a welcome respite, that nagging injury you had and could train through when you were in shape may give you more trouble when you're not fit. The body's natural painkillers are not up to their former level.

9

On Race Strategy, Tactics and Transition

In many ways, the triathlon is like a war — it's an athlete's personal struggle against physical exhaustion, injury, the elements and mechanical failure. His overall plan (strategy), execution (tactics) and preparedness (logistics) will influence how well he does. A sound plan can reduce the chances of making a critical mistake; a faulty plan can mean the big DNF — Did Not Finish. Carl von Clausewitz, the renowned Prussian military strategist of the 19th century, would have enjoyed planning a strategy for the triathlon. He would have found it a worthy opponent.

The goal of every triathlete falls into one of three categories: to finish, to improve time and/or to win. The strategy for finishing is different from that of improving time or winning. Once you decide on a goal, ask yourself if you are properly trained to go after it. If you have the athletic ability of a banana slug, forget about winning. In deciding on strategy, ask yourself questions like these: Is it a short or long event? Is it in hot or cold weather? What is the order of events? And don't let the excitement of the moment divert your attention from the task at hand; stick to your game plan throughout the race.

Finishing is Half the Battle

In my first triathlon, the Ironman, my goal was simply to finish. I had no grand illusions about winning. I vowed that I would pace myself through the three events and compete only against myself, not others. Pace in a long triathlon is about as

116

important as remembering to bring your suntan lotion to the beach. If you don't, you get burned.

Here's the strategy: Swim well within your limits. Ride hard, but don't go into oxygen debt. Run at a pace that will assure finishing and does not risk injury.

Your first triathlon should be your personal struggle. Without the pressure of doing well, you can pick up tactics and logistics and get a better feel for the event. By setting a modest goal for yourself, you are less likely to be disappointed by not finishing. Sometimes, however, the DNF can be a tremendous incentive to return and do it right next time. Most triathletes who don't finish the Ironman swear on a stack of Bibles that they'll be back next year. In most cases, they've either trained improperly or chosen the wrong strategy.

Improving Time and Winning

Rather than looking at a triathlon as a winning or losing proposition, think of it as an opportunity to improve your time. If you can complete the race in a time that is close to a previous winning effort, setting a time goal is a natural step to winning without the added pressure of winning.

Here is the winning strategy: Swim as hard as you can so you're not too far behind the first person out of the water. Once on the bicycle, establish your position. In the run, secure or improve your position.

Swim: You can throw away your arms after the swim, so swim hard, but don't push yourself into oxygen debt. The kick is not too important, so keep the legs fresh for the bike ride by avoiding a lot of kicking.

Bike: A lot of competitive triathletes make the mistake of holding back in the ride. They think that saving their energy will give them a faster run. Wrong. The energy saved by riding at a slower speed is merely time lost — you can't make it up in the run even if you do have a little more energy.

For the sake of argument, let's say that a cyclist decides to ride conservatively, about 15 minutes slower than he is capable of. At the Ironman, that 15 minutes is the difference between riding at 19 mph and 20 mph. And the difference in energy output between the two speeds doesn't amount to more than a hill of refried beans. You've simply lost that time before the run and you're never going to make it up.

Run: There are three basic strategies: starting out fast and hanging on, starting slowly and picking up the pace or running at an even pace throughout. I prefer the latter. In the last stage of

Once out of the water, know where to go to find your gear.

the triathlon, you must keep yourself motivated, and I know of no better way to do so than to pass fellow triathletes. Key on the runner in front of you, and once you get up to him, pass him with a short burst of speed, enough to place some distance between the two of you. Then turn your attention to the next runner ahead.

Ultimately, planning a strategy for a triathlon — and its outcome — may depend to some extent on how evenly balanced the distances are. In the USTS races, for example, I think the swimmer has a slight advantage. First, he can show his stuff immediately. He can get out in front of the pack and away from slower swimmers who would otherwise get in his way and slow him down. Second, the 40-kilometer bicycle ride and 15-kilometer run aren't enough to allow a strong cyclist or runner to catch up to a good swimmer who is a satisfactory runner and cyclist.

At the Ironman, however, even though most claim that the bike ride is too long and the swim too short, I think the distances are well-balanced. A good swimmer can put as much as 30 minutes between himself and a mediocre swimmer who is a good cyclist or runner. In the bike ride, the gap between a good swimmer or runner cycling at 19 mph and a great rider cycling at 21 mph, will only be about 35 minutes, even after 112 miles. Finally, in the marathon, the best runner in the world won't be able to do much better than 2:45 after a hard ride, and yet the best cyclist or swimmer who has no running background can still muster a 3:15. No matter how you cut it, the time gap will be about 30 minutes.

GREMLINS, CRAP SHOOTING AND ACES WILD

Let's face it: Sometimes you can't predict some situations, like three flats in one race or your bike frame breaking midway through the ride. However, you do have a few weapons to use in the battle against the elements, physical exhaustion, injury and even mechanical failure.

The Elements

Race officials do everything they can to reduce the risks of excessive heat or cold in a triathlon. An alternate date for the Ironman is always scheduled in the event of heavy rains, and USTS races are held in the summer early in the morning when temperatures are cool and lakes warm. There are no written guarantees though, so be prepared for the worst. Here are some specific situations you need to think about.

PROBLEM: Cold-water swim. *Strategy:* This is no time to be taking it easy, so swim at a brisk pace. *Tactics:* Wear a protective rubber swim cap to retain body heat. Some triathletes go so far as to smear their bodies with lanolin or Vaseline. Recognize signs of hypothermia: numb limbs, inability to think quickly, a sense of euphoria, drowsiness, loss of coordination. At the Malibu Triathlon, Mark Allen, hardly more than 100 feet from shore, said that he couldn't figure out how to get there because the cold ocean water had scrambled his mental faculties. Race officials wisely pulled him from the race when, after reaching shore, he couldn't figure out where the bicycles were, even though they were right in front of him.

PROBLEM: Poor road conditions. *Strategy:* Ride conservatively. *Tactics:* Ride on heavier tires to minimize the greater risk of flatting. Carry two spare tubes or sew-up tires. Train on dirt roads before the race.

PROBLEM: Hot weather. *Strategy:* Slow down in the run and ride. Recognize symptoms of heat exhaustion: cool, moist feeling on your face; pale, cool, clammy skin; weak, rapid pulse; shallow respiration; tense, contracted muscles. *Tactics:* Train in heat to do well in heat.

Physical Exhaustion

PROBLEM: Can't finish swim. *Strategy:* Float on back, raise your hand to signal for help. Don't panic. *Tactics:* More training.

PROBLEM: Tired in bike ride. *Strategy:* Rest at the bike/run transition and assess ability to continue. Increase intake of liquids and food. *Tactics:* Push easier gear and slow down.

PROBLEM: Fatigue in run. *Strategy:* Concentrate on pace. Monitor body. *Tactics:* Key on other runners. Walk only as a last resort.

Injury

At the first sign of injury, the best thing you can do is pull out and save yourself for another day. Pat Hines had other ideas in her second Ironman in 1982. In the February edition, she led until midway in the run when she was stopped by a stress fracture. In the October race, the story was similar. Rather than dropping out, she threw caution to the wind and walked the rest of the marathon, which took her more than nine hours. Dave Horning has swallowed his pride twice at the Ironman and dropped out because of exhaustion from the heat. He recognized the symptoms of heat exhaustion and dehydration in time to avoid a disaster.

Mechanical Failure

PROBLEM: Flat tire. *Strategy:* Pre-race preparation. I wouldn't believe it if I hadn't seen it at Hawaii with my own eyes. A triathlete riding on sew-ups flatted and didn't know how to change the tire. He'd never even had a flat before! If you haven't flatted before your first triathlon, you should at least know how to change a tube or sew-up. Also, carry a bike pump and know how to use it.

PROBLEM: Mechanical failure. *Strategy:* Check out bike before race. *Tactics:* Monitor bike during race. The reckless triathlete's bicycle is dirty and has a squeaky chain. He relies on Monty Python's "Bicycle Repairman" for help. The well-prepared triathlete's bike is finely tuned and checked out by a mechanic a week before the race. He knows the fundamentals of bike mechanics.

TACTICS

Talking and training with experienced triathletes is the best way I know of to pick up tactics. After finishing fourth at the Ironman, I have received calls from triathletes around the country who want to know how to train and what to expect in a race.

Here are just a few tactics I've learned over the past two years:

1) Open-water swimming often involves competing in f-i-l-t-h-y water. In one race, I saw triathletes competing in water the color of pea soup, accompanied by dead fish and rotting tires. Be sure you have had your tetanus shot and avoid swallowing the slime.

2) Familiarize yourself with the course and keep track of your splits in all three events.

3) Check in or register for the race the moment you arrive.

4) If you have a special food or drink, place it on the course where you'll need it most.

5) Know where to exit the water. Triathletes are sometimes led astray by spectators on the shore who might not be at the right exit area.

6) Drafting during the swim is not only legal, it's highly recommended. You can save a lot of energy by following another swimmer's wake and not having to look up to see where you're going.

Be sure your number is pinned on before the start of the tri-athlon.

7) Put your bike in low gear before the race. When leaving the transition area, you can thus accelerate quickly.

8) Have spare clothing tied to your handlebars, if you feel you're going to be cold from the swim or from the weather.

9) Release both toe straps before entering the transition area so that you can dismount quickly.

10) Double-lace your shoes so that they won't come untied. For some mysterious reason, triathletes have a habit of misplacing their running shoes. Know where they are.

LOGISTICS

Logistical foul-ups have lost wars and made fools of generals. Without sufficient ammunition, food and water, an army — no matter how powerful on paper — can turn into a helpless mob ripe for defeat. The poorly prepared triathlete is asking for a drubbing. Enter a triathlon without clothing, race number, bicycle, helmet, shoes, swimsuit or swim cap and you can forget about finishing. And there are a host of other items that, although nonessential, can make your triathlon seem like the Bataan Death March without them.

Why not play it safe and make a checklist? My list is broken down into three levels based on importance: Essential — You can't play the game without it; Highly Recommended — You're playing Russian Roulette, with three bullets; Optional — You never planned on needing it until the one time it saved you from having to drop out.

ESSENTIAL

1. bicycle	5. running shoes
2. entry number and race information	6. swim cap
3. swimsuit	7. running shorts, bike clothing

HIGHLY RECOMMENDED

1. goggles	8. socks
2. Vaseline	9. cycle gloves
3. suntan lotion	10. cycle shoes
4. cycle jersey	11. long-sleeve shirt
5. frame-mounted pump	12. two water bottles
6. spare inner tubes or sew-ups	13. two tire irons
7. cycle shorts with chamois	14. chain rivet extractor

OPTIONAL

1. beach towel
2. first-aid kit
3. cloth tape
4. heating pad
5. long-sleeve wool jersey
6. wool cycling tights and cap

7. rearview mirror
8. bicycle spokes
9. spoke wrench
10. spare tires and wheels
11. tire pump — floor model
12. watch

TRANSITION

The transition area is a triathlete's pit stop and one aspect of the race that makes it unique in sports. How many sports are there where being a quick-change artist is an asset? Some triathletes can change clothing in less than a minute.

The atmosphere in the transition area is about as close to organized mayhem as you can get. Triathletes are busy washing off saltwater, changing clothes, applying suntan lotion, fixing bike gear, yelling to friends on the sidelines, even kissing their babies goodbye. Siga Albrecht did just that at the Ironman one year when both she and her husband, Hans, competed and finished. In the bike/run transition, triathletes come bearing down on the change area like stock cars at the Firecracker 500 — tires skidding, lungs puffing like high-performance engines. And nine times out of 10, there is that triathlete who can't find his gear and walks around like a lost soul in search of salvation.

At many triathlons, handlers or outside assistance of any kind is illegal. Race officials coordinate your gear throughout the event, which has its advantages and disadvantages. You don't have to think about your gear once you've dropped it off, but there's always the chance that officials will misplace your gear. Whatever the situation, be sure you know where your gear will be or where it's supposed to be. If you've got a number, don't forget what it is, and shout it out to officials when you arrive to change.

While most triathlon courses provide a secluded changing area, some triathletes forego the luxury and change clothes right next to their bikes. If you choose this procedure, realize that the bikes are often parked in an empty lot where you'll be eyeballed by spectators. At the San Francisco USTS race, though, that didn't deter many men or women from saving precious seconds.

Under normal conditions, your transition time should be between two and three minutes. If you take longer, perhaps you should practice changing clothes. Do you stuff your socks into your shoes? Are your cycling gloves difficult to put on? Do you wear a one-piece cycling suit that doesn't fit? Do you get flustered easily? The excitement of competition can get your blood pumping and, although you should maintain that racer's edge, you don't want to blow it and lose your cool in transition.

I can't stress enough the importance of the transition area for assessing your physical condition. Medical aid, food and water will be available there. If you're feeling sick, that's the place to sit back and take stock. Out on the course, medical help might be an hour or more away.

Race Autopsy

You'll probably feel dead after your triathlon, so it's a great time to conduct the post-race autopsy. Don't bury the bad memories. You can gain a lot by collecting your thoughts after the race and asking yourself where your training could improve, where you made mistakes in the race and where you did the right things. I like to write down my thoughts while they're still fresh. Did I maintain the proper pace throughout? Did my bike handle well? Where should I train harder to get the most improvement?

Finally, after a triathlon, why not let the race director know what you thought of the race? If you think the course could stand change, tell him. Point out the strong points of the race as well as the places where it could be improved. Always think along the lines of safety. Meet directors are generally busy with a thousand little details after the race, so write a letter rather than make your suggestions immediately. Anything you do to make the triathlon more enjoyable and safe will help assure the sport's future in America.

Appendix

SAMPLE DIARY

The following excerpt from the diary of budding triathlete, Zachary Minimus, illustrates the value of recording workouts. Minimus has decided to enter his first triathlon, the USTS in San Francisco, on July 10. Zack, as you may recall, is a veteran marathon runner. He needs to work on both his swimming and his cycling. Here are four pages from his workout diary, one week for each training phase.

PHASE 1

Sunday (April 18): Swam 2000 yards in the morning. It was my first time at that distance. I felt pretty comfortable. I rode 30 miles in the afternoon at an easy pace.

Monday (April 19): Went for an early swim at the local masters club pool — 1000 yards. Ran 10 miles after work over rolling terrain. Calves sore from bike ride Sunday.

Tuesday (April 20): Took morning off. Went on an easy 30-mile bike ride after work. Calves felt better.

Wednesday (April 21): Swam 2 x 500 yards before work, with a five-minute rest between sets. After work ran eight miles at an easy pace.

Thursday (April 22): Swam 1000 yards at lunchtime. Rode 20 miles after work and immediately got off the bike and ran four miles. Felt strange; it'll take some getting used to.

Friday (April 23): Day off. Slept in.

Saturday (April 24): My coach watched me swim 1000 yards. I need more extension of the hand before entry, but otherwise it's all coming together. Relatively easy swim. I ran 15 miles in the afternoon with three other triathletes. Running with a group sure made the miles go easier.

Week Total:	Swim	6000 yards
	Bike	80 miles
	Run	37 miles

PHASE 2

Sunday (May 16): Swam 5 x 200 yards with 15 seconds rest between sets. Better extension according to coach, but left and right arms aren't symmetrical during the complete stroke. Right arm seems to be wandering too far out midway through the pull. After swim, rode a 30-kilometer time-trial. Fastest time yet.

Monday (May 17): Easy 1000-yard swim before work. Ran 10 miles after work — 2-mile warmup, 6 x 1 mile at 15 seconds under race pace with 880 jog/rest and then a 2-mile warmdown.

Tuesday (May 18): Very little time to work out today. Did a one-hour all-out ride during lunch. Covered more than 18 miles.

Wednesday (May 19): Hard morning swim, 20 x 100 yards. Did 10 x 100 yards with hand paddles and pull buoy, and 10 without while coach watched and commented between each set. Ran 10 miles after work at a fairly brisk pace. Feel like it's time for a day off.

Thursday (May 20): Day off.

Friday (May 21): No morning swim. Rode 30 miles in the hills after work. Did some intervals on the track — one-mile warm-up run, 6 x 880 yards all-out and one-mile warmdown. Achilles tendon bothering me.

Saturday (May 22): Swam 5 x 200 yards with 15 seconds rest between sets. Then went for an easy 10-mile run. Achilles tendon felt better. Maybe the swim helped.

Week Total:	Swim	5000 yards
	Bike	67 miles
	Run	35 miles

PHASE 3

Sunday (June 20): Easy two-kilometer swim; 40-kilometer time trial. Then an easy three-mile run to warm down and get better feel for hard ride to run transition. That distance and combination felt comfortable.

Monday (June 21): Well-deserved day off. Although I feel great, the past few days have been real quality days. This rest will assure that I don't get sick.

Tuesday (June 22): Morning swim of 4 x 500 yards using pull buoy and hand paddles. Feel my form coming together. Ran 10 miles after work with a friend.

Wednesday (June 23): Took the day off from work to get in a 40-mile ride over hilly terrain. Felt strong. Ran four miles immediately afterward.

Thursday (June 24): Easy 1000-yard swim before work. Ran 10 miles after work at slightly slower than race pace.

Friday (June 25): Rode 30 miles hard, then ran a 10-kilometer course hard at race pace. Very satisfied with the transition time and finally comfortable with the muscles used in cycling and running.

Saturday (June 26): Felt tired and decided to take a day off. I'm in great shape now, so a day off won't matter.

	Week Total:	Swim	5150 yards
		Bike	95 miles
		Run	33 miles

PHASE 4

Sunday (July 4): 40-mile ride. Last hard workout before race. Felt a little tired. Went to see fireworks with girlfriend.

Monday (July 5): Swam 500 yards and ran six miles.

Tuesday (July 6): Swam 400 yards, rode 15 miles and then ran two miles.

Wednesday (July 7): Ran seven miles after work. Feeling stronger and ready to race.

Thursday (July 8): Swam 400 yards and rode 10 miles real easy. Went to bed at 9 p.m. to get rest. Know tomorrow will be hectic.

Friday (July 9): Ran two miles just to keep my sanity. All week I've felt guilty about not training. Went to bed at 11 p.m., but didn't get to sleep until 1 a.m.

Saturday (July 10): RACE.

Week Total:	Swim	1300 yards
	Bike	65 miles
	Run	17 miles

What follows is a hypothetical training diary leading up to the October Hawaii Ironman Triathlon. Zachary is intent on finishing under 12:00. As you read the diary, you will pick up on what thoughts go through the triathlete's mind as he trains. This is a more important consideration than mileage.

TRAINING DIARY
PHASE 1

MAY 16 - 22: Last few weeks of Phase 1 training. Getting very comfortable with Category 1 workouts. Feeling more comfortable swimming longer distances and my running legs have finally adapted to cycling. Anxious to begin doing some speedwork soon, but I recognize the need to continue building a strong base in all three sports.

Sunday (May 16): Swim: 1000 yards. Ride: 60 miles. Swam 1000 yards easy (no time). Took about five minutes to dry off and change. Then rode 60 miles in rolling hills in about 3:45. The transition from swimming to cycling feels better than previous workouts.

Monday (May 17): Swim: 2500 yards. Run: 15 miles. Five sets of 500s in 9:30 with 30 seconds rest between, before work. Ran 15 miles at 7:20 pace after work. Felt good to run that much since I've been concentrating more on swimming and cycling recently.

Tuesday (May 18): Swim: 1500 yards. Ride: 50 miles. No morning workout today. Felt I needed the extra recovery from previous three days, although I plan to rest tomorrow. Swam 1500 yards non-stop in 29:20 (after work). Immediately rode 50 miles on a flat course.

Wednesday (May 19): Rest. I spent about 30 minutes stretching while watching the evening news.

Thursday (May 20): Swim: 1500 yards. Ride: 45 miles. Met with the swim coach this morning. Did 15 x 100 yards at medium effort while she watched and commented between intervals. Says I'm still tight in my shoulders and this is hurting my reach during stroke. After work rode 45 miles; took more than 3½ hours because of two flats. At least I'm getting the tube change down.

Friday (May 21): Ride: 30 miles. Run: 10 miles. After work rode 30 miles easy and immediately ran 10 miles at a relatively slow pace. The transition still feels awkward and it takes about three miles to feel like I'm running smoothly. The legs might be tired from this relatively high-mileage week. Think I'll take it easier tomorrow and rest for a good long ride on Sunday.

Saturday (May 22): Swim: 3000 yards. Felt great this morning but decided to go easy on the legs as planned. Swam 3000 yards (3 x 1000) in an hour, then lay out in the sun all day.

Week Total:	Swim	9500 yards
	Bike	185 miles
	Run	25 miles

PHASE 2

JULY 11 - 17: Sixth week of Phase 2. The more I mix in the Category 2 workouts, the stronger I feel, but it takes longer to recover from workouts. Knees feel stronger and able to push bigger gears now. Much stronger and more confident in the water, also. Getting used to running slower.

Sunday (July 11): Ride: 50 miles. Run: 10 miles. Rode 50 miles over hilly terrain with the guys from the bike shop. Really a fartlek workout because we raced to the top of each hill and coasted down the backsides. Riding with better cyclists forces me to push bigger gears. After the ride I immediately went for a 10-mile run and felt surprisingly good. Transition was smooth and I felt good right away.

Monday (July 12): Swim: 2500 yards. Easy day. Swam 2500 yards in the morning. After a 500-yard warmup, I did 8 x 200 yards with hand paddles and pull buoys. Twenty seconds rest between each, then a 400-yard warmdown.

Tuesday (July 13): Swim: 2000 yards. Ride: 20 miles. Run: 5 miles. Swam 2000 easy before work. After work did a very hard one-hour ride. Stayed in the big chainwheel the entire time. Felt good to go anaerobic and to be able to recover quickly. Finished the ride at the track and then did 5 x 1 miles in 7:30 with a half-mile walk/jog between.

Wednesday (July 14): Ride: 20 miles. Run: 10 miles. Rested in the morning. Rode easy 20 after work and immediately ran 10 miles in the hills.

Thursday (July 15): Swim 3000 yards. Ride: 30 miles. Swam with the coach this morning. Basically everything looks good in the pool. I feel like I've patterned an efficient stroke and my times are improving steadily. Did 30 x 100 yards with a 15-second rest between them. After work rode 30 miles hard in a fartlek-type workout. Sprinted up the hills and coasted down them.

Friday (July 16): Rest. Pulse was high this morning. Have had a few days of hard work so a day off won't hurt.

Saturday (July 17): Swim: 1000 yards. Ride: 40 miles. Run: 10 miles. Swam 1000 yards easy, then rode 40 miles at race pace and ran 10 miles in about 80 minutes. Felt like a real triathlete.

Week Total:	Swim	8500 yards
	Bike	160 miles
	Run	35 miles

PHASE 3

SEPTEMBER 12 - 18: All coming together now. Four 100-mile rides under my belt, and several 2.4-mile pool swims. Feeling faster and stronger all the time. Slight foot problem running so have cut down mileage. Will only run after riding or swimming. I need a long run (about 20 miles) before the Ironman. Maybe Tuesday or Wednesday.

Sunday (September 12): Ride: 100 miles. Run: 4 miles. Did a great 100-mile ride today, alone, in six hours. No food, just water. Pretty hilly course. Concentrated and focused the entire ride. Started to bonk around 85 miles but hung in there. Felt terrible when I got home but managed to put on running shoes and go four miles. Felt better at end than I did at beginning of run.

Monday (September 13): Rest.

Tuesday (September 14): Swim: 4224 yards. Ride: 20 miles. Swam time trial this morning 2.4 miles in pool. Took 81 minutes. Rode 20 miles easy afterward.

Wednesday (September 15): Ride: 20 miles. Run 20 miles. Took the morning easy; slept late. After work did a 20-mile ride and a 20-mile run. This may be my last long run before the race. Felt better than I anticipated.

Thursday (September 16): Swim: 2500 yards. Noon swim 2500 yards (5 x 500 at race pace). Easy day.

Friday (September 17): Ride: 60 miles. Run: 10 miles. Rode a very hilly 60 miles as hard as I could. Immediately ran 10 miles at 7:20 pace.

Saturday (September 18): Time trial. Swim: 2000 yards. Ride: 30 miles. Run: 5 miles. Swam 2000 yards in 19 minutes; rode 30 miles in 1:40; ran 5 miles in 38:00. Will take day off tomorrow.

Week Total:	Swim	8724 yards
	Bike	230 miles
	Run	39 miles

PHASE 4

OCTOBER 2 - 8: Ready as I'll ever be. The work is done and now it is a matter of resting. I feel I've reached my potential and now I hope to store up some mental reserves to call on during the race. Arrived in Hawaii last night (Friday, October 1) very excited. Try not to overwork.

Saturday (October 2): Ride: 50 miles. Run: 10 miles. Rode 50 miles over part of course and got a feel for the first and last sections. Ran 10 miles in the afternoon. Very easy run with friends.

Sunday (October 3): Swim: 2000 yards. Ride: 20 miles. Swam 2000 yards in the ocean. Actually it was out to a large sailboat and back, but it felt like 2000 yards. Wanted to get used to the waves and the taste of saltwater. Water was warm. Rode 20 miles immediately after swim.

Monday (October 4): Swim: 1000 yards. Run: 8 miles. Swam about 1000 yards in the ocean today. Ran 8 miles easy this afternoon. Heat doesn't seem to bother me. Am carbohydrate-loading.

Tuesday (October 5): 20-mile ride.

Wednesday (October 6): 500-yard swim.

Thursday (October 7): 15-mile ride.

Friday (October 8): 10-mile ride, just to keep from going crazy.

Saturday (October 9): RACE!

Week Total:	Swim	3500 yards
	Bike	115 miles
	Run	18 miles

SWIMMING PACE CHART
DISTANCE

Pace Min./100 yd.	1000 meters (.62 miles)	1 mile	1.2 miles	2000 meters (1.24 miles)	2.4 miles
1:00	10:56	17:36	21:07	21:52	42:14
1:05	11:51	19:04	22:53	23:42	45:46
1:10	12:46	20:32	24:38	25:32	49:16
1:15	13:41	22:00	26:24	27:22	52:48
1:20	14:35	23:28	28:08	29:10	56:19
1:25	15:30	24:56	29:55	31:00	59:50
1:30	16:25	26:24	31:41	32:50	1:03:22
1:35	17:19	27:52	33:26	34:38	1:06:53
1:40	18:14	29:20	35:12	36:28	1:10:24
1:50	20:03	32:16	38:43	40:06	1:17:26
2:00	21:53	35:12	42:14	43:46	1:24:29
2:10	23:42	38:08	45:46	46:24	1:31:31
2:20	25:31	41:04	49:17	51:02	1:38:34
2:30	27:21	44:00	52:48	54:42	1:45:36
2:40	29:10	46:56	56:19	58:20	1:52:38
2:50	31:00	49:52	59:50	1:05:39	1:59:41
3:00	32:49	52:48	1:03:22	1:02:00	2:06:43

CYCLING PACE CHART
DISTANCE

M.P.H.	40-K	56 miles	100 miles	112 miles
10	2:29	5:36	10:00	11:12
11	2:16	5:05:30	9:06	10:11
12	2:05	4:40	8:19	9:20
13	1:54	4:18	7:42	8:36
14	1:46	4:00	7:08	8:00
15	1:40	3:44	6:40	7:28
16	1:33	3:30	6:15	7:00
17	1:28	3:17:30	5:53	6:35
18	1:23	3:06:30	5:33	6:13
19	1:18	2:57	5:15	5:54
20	1:14	2:48	5:00	5:36
21	1:11	2:39:30	4:45	5:19
22	1:08	2:33	4:33	5:06
23	1:05	2:26	4:21	4:52
24	1:01	2:20	4:09	4:40
25	:59	2:14:30	4:00	4:29

If you know your average speed, this pace chart can help you determine your overall time in the triathlon. If you average 16 mph for 112 miles, you take 7 hours. Note how time improves markedly with an increase of only 1 mph for 112 miles. As you can see, the triathlete can improve his time the most in the bike ride because it takes up a greater proportion of the triathlon than the swim and run.

RUNNING PACE CHART
DISTANCE

Average Pace Minutes / Mile	10-K	15-K	13.1-mile	26.2-mile
15:00				6:33
14:00			3:03	6:06
13:00			2:51	5:42
12:00			2:37	5:15
11:00		1:42:45	2:24	4:48
10:00	1:02:18	1:33:24	2:11	4:22
9:45	1:00:42	1:31:03	2:08	4:15
9:30	59:12	1:28:42	2:05	4:09
9:00	56:05	1:24:03	1:58	3:56
8:45	54:30	1:21:42	1:54	3:49
8:30	52:57	1:19:24	1:52	3:43
8:15	51:24	1:17:03	1:48	3:36
8:00	49:50	1:14:42	1:45	3:30
7:45	48:17	1:12:24	1:42	3:23
7:30	46:42	1:10:03	1:39	3:17
7:15	45:12	1:07:42	1:35	3:10
7:00	43:36	1:05:24	1:31:45	3:03:33
6:45	42:05	1:03:03	1:28	2:57
6:30	40:30	1:00:42	1:25	2:50
6:15	39:00	58:24	1:21	
6:00	37:25	56:03	1:18	
5:30	34:15	51:21	1:12	
5:15	32:45	49:06	1:09	

IMPORTANT CONTACTS FOR THE TRIATHLETE

United States Triathlon Association
P.O. Box 7798
Burbank, CA 91510
(213) 483-6181

United States Cycling Federation
1750 East Boulder
Colorado Springs, CO 80909
(303) 632-5551

The Athletics Congress (running)
155 W. Washington St.
Suite 200
Indianapolis, IN 46204
(317) 638-9155

U.S. Swimming, Inc.
1750 E. Boulder St.
Colorado Springs, CO 80909
(303) 578-4578

United States Triathlon Series
Endurance Sports Productions
507 F. St.
Davis, CA 95616
(916) 758-9868

Hawaii Ironman Triathlon
P.O. Box 25861
Honolulu, HI 96825
(808) 395-5163

Bibliography

Bailey, Covert. *Fit or Fat?*. Boston: Houghton Mifflin Company, 1977.

Boyle, Robert H. *Sport – Mirror of American Life.* Boston: Little, Brown and Company, 1963.

Cavanagh, Peter. *The Running Shoe Book.* Mountain View, Calif.: Anderson World Publications, 1980.

Complete Bicycle Time Trialing Book, by the editors of *Bike World* magazine. Mountain View, Calif.: World Publications, 1977.

Costill, David L. *A Scientific Approach to Distance Running.* Los Altos, Calif.: *Track and Field News,* 1979.

George, Barbara, ed. *Inside the Cyclist.* Brattleboro, Vt.: *Velo-news,* 1975.

Goldstein, Avram. "Endorphins." *The Sciences,* Vol. 18, No. 3, pp. 14 - 19.

The Healing Arts. Stanford, Calif.: Stanford University Publications, No. 1, 1977, p. 8.

Karlgaard, Richard. *The Last Word on Running.* Ottawa, Ill.: Caroline House Publishers, 1978.

Kyle, Chester. "Go With the Flow, Aerodynamics and Cycling." *Bicycling.* May 1982. pp. 59 - 66.

Lilliefors, Jim. *The Running Mind.* Mountain View, Calif.: World Publications, 1978.

Matheny, Fred. *Beginning Bicycle Racing.* Brattleboro, Vt.: *Velo-news,* 1980.

Michener, James. *Sports in America.* New York: Random House, 1976.

The Runner's Diet, by the editors of *Runner's World* magazine. Mountain View, Calif.: World Publications, 1972.

Sobey, Ed, and Burns, Gary. *Runner's World Aerobic Weight Training Book.* Mountain View, Calif.: Runner's World Books, 1982.

Swim, Bike, Run, "1982 National Triathlon Calendar." *Swim Swim.* Spring 1982, pp. 9 - 15.

About the Authors

Mark Sisson was born and raised in Maine; he attended the Phillips Exeter Academy in New Hampshire and Williams College in Massachusetts, where he developed a strong interest in exercise physiology and received a Bachelor of Science degree in biology.

Always interested in new challenges, Sisson, 30, has been a scuba diver, sky diver, mountain climber, hang glider and airplane pilot; he has done all of this while competing as a national-class marathon runner and triathlete. When not training, the self-employed entrepreneur finds time to manage two businesses. Sisson lives in Menlo Park, California.

Ray Hosler was born in Louisiana and raised in Colorado and Wyoming; he attended Colorado State University, where he received a Bachelor of Arts degree in journalism.

Hosler has worked for two daily newspapers, *Runner's World* magazine, and is presently the senior book editor at Anderson World Publications in Mountain View, California.

His interests in sports include running, cycling, backpacking, cross-country skiing, racquetball and swimming. He has been a competitive marathon runner and bike racer.

Recommended Reading

MAGAZINES

Triathlon Magazine, 8461 Warner Drive, Culver City, CA 90230. (213) 558-3321. Quarterly. Editor: Penny Little. The first issue, *Swim-Bike-Run,* was printed in 1982 as a calendar of triathlons. The first official issue was printed in February 1983, including race coverage, columns, a national calendar and features by top triathletes.

Runner's World, P.O. Box 366, Mountain View, CA 94042. (415) 965-8777. Editor and publisher: Bob Anderson. 13 times annually. This glossy, full-color publication covers running from A to Z. Several training articles on the triathlon by well-known triathletes have appeared. Other topics on running: training, diet, racing, health, stretching, calendar of events.

Swim Swim, 8461 Warner Drive, Culver City, CA 90230. (213) 558-3321. Editor: Penny Little. Quarterly. Although short on training articles and technique tips, this publication offers a complete listing of masters swim programs. Articles are written by well-known swimmers, such as Marianne Brems and Bruce Furniss.

Swimming World Magazine and Junior Swimmer, P.O. Box 45497, Los Angeles, CA 90045. Monthly. A glossy magazine that gives training tips, along with stories about personalities and events. Race results, calendar of events, photos and columns by noted swimmers and coaches.

Bicycling, 33 E. Minor St., Emmaus, PA 38049. (215) 967-5171. Editor: James C. McCullagh. 9 times annually. This is the country's biggest glossy, quality cycling publication. Rodale Press does a commendable job covering the sport and occasionally includes stories on the triathlon. Article subjects include: safety, diet, technique, new products, new bikes, repair, stories, touring, racing, calendar of events.

Velo-news, A Journal of Bicycle Racing, Box 1257, Brattleboro, VT 05301. (301) 254-2305. Editor: Barbara George. 18 issues per year. Covering primarily U.S. amateur racing, this news tabloid also delves into training tips and new-product reviews. Provides a calendar of upcoming bike races and classified ads for used bikes.

BOOKS

Teach Yourself to Swim Despite Your Fear of Water by Mick Arellano. One of the best books on teaching swimming to the adult who has a fear of water. Instructions are written for the person desiring to learn alone in shallow water, at his own pace. Hardback, 142 pages. Hawthorn Books, Inc.

The All New Complete Book of Bicycling by Eugene A. Sloane. This revised and expanded edition is one of the most complete books published on bicycling. Everything you need to know about frames, components, clothing, repairs, wheel building, and training. Hardbound, 736 pages. Simon and Schuster.

Inside the Cyclist, by *Velo-news.* This collection of articles published in past issues of *Velo-news* is loaded with important training information on physiology and diet. Oriented toward the bike racer. Paperback, 128 pages.

Glenn's Complete Bicycle Manual by Clarence W. Coles and Harold T. Glenn. The only definitive textbook on bicycle maintenance. It's loaded with excellent photos showing all the steps in a complete overhaul of a ten-speed, plus schematics of parts like hubs, bottom brackets, etc. Paperback, 339 pages, Crown Publishers, Inc.

Anybody's Bike Book by Tom Cuthbertson. The "little brother" of *Glenn's* repair manual, Cuthbertson has written a repair book for the novice cyclist in a humorous and easy-to-follow style. The illustrations alone are worth the price. Paperback, 175 pages, Ten Speed Press.

Jog, Run, Race by Joe Henderson. A landmark book in guiding the novice runner from walking to jogging to running to racing. Henderson writes with a captivating, conversational style that inspires as well as informs. Must reading for the beginner. Paperback, 201 pages, Anderson World Books.

Runner's World Aerobic Weight Training Book by Edwin Sobey and Gary Burns. A complete view of weight training through elaborate aerobic exercise programs. To complement bicycling, gymnastics, canoeing — the whole gamut. Paperback, $ 9.95

Runner's World Massage Book by Ray Hosler. A down-to-earth guide to body massage that treats the physiological as well as the psychological and philosophical. Paperback, $ 9.95

Runner's World Advanced Indoor Exercise Book by Richard Benyo and Rhonda Provost. For committed exercisers — an extensive program for body strengthening and flexibility. Paperback, $ 9.95

Runner's World Stretching Book by Nell Weaver. A new approach to conditioning incorporating flexibility, speed, balance, agility, coordination, endurance and grace. Paperback, $ 9.95

Runner's World Vitamin Book by Virginia DeMoss. From Vitamin A to Zinc — consumers are offered an inside report on this ever-increasing market. Spiral-bound, $ 11.95

Available in fine bookstores and sport shops, or from:

Runner's World Books

P.O. Box 159, Mountain View, CA 94042

Include $ 1.00 shipping and handling for each title (maximum $ 3.00)